TABLE OF CONTENTS

iv

PREFACE

TRENDS AND ISSUES AFFECTING CURRICULUM:
PROGRAMS AND PRACTICES is provided as a guide to
all educators on the job and graduate students in
education. It enables one to gain an overall
perspective on professional literature. It is a
quick reference guide for the desk of the person
who wants an insight into current developments in
education. The authors seek to inform the readers
as to what is taking place on the educational
scene, not to classify trends on any value scale.

This publication provides a synopsis of
trends and issues as identified by the authors
through a study of articles from twenty professional journals. It is designed to acquaint the
reader with ideas, experimentations, and innovations
to the extent that certain trends are recognizable.
Changing emphases in content areas, skills areas,
organizational procedures, and techniques are
presented which seem to affect the curriculum.

The mode of presentation is a set of trend
topics supported by an overview, a set of synopses,
and a list of references for each trend. The
trend topics provide a frame of reference for
the publication. The synopses of journal articles
offer descriptions of situations and studies
relevant to the respective topics. A list of
descriptors for each topic aids in determining
the trend's scope. Each descriptor is related to
at least one article synopsis in the chapter to
which it is attached.

The overview for each chapter enables the
reader to attain a brief perspective of the trend
area and the supporting data. It provides the
major points of view and the emphases peculiar to
programs and practices presented in the journal
articles cited in the respective chapter.

The body of chapters two through ten is
composed of synopses of articles which support the

existence of each respective trend as seen by the
authors. Each synopsis gives only that information
which appears relevant to the trend statement.
No attempt is made to provide a complete digest
of any article. It is anticipated that the
brief synopses will assist the reader in selecting
articles for reading from original sources.

Articles, for which synopses are provided
in this publication, were chosen by the authors
from selections made by teachers, supervisors,
and administrators engaged in graduate study in
the College of Education of the University of
Georgia and from the readings of the authors of
this publication. Criteria for selecting each
article includes: 1) articles published within
the last three years in a journal which is the
official organ of a professional education
organization or a professional education institution, 2) articles which reflect a trend
affecting the curriculum, and 3) articles
considered helpful to educators in selecting
an innovation for implementation in a school.

Recognition and appreciation are extended
to all who contributed to the production of this
publication. Special recognition is given to
all graduate students of the University of Georgia
who submitted synopses of journal articles for
consideration in ECS 704, "Trends and Issues in
Curriculum." We are especially grateful to the
secretaries and graduate assistants Linda Edwards,
Lawana Slocumbe, Warren Schollaert, and Frank
Faust at the University of Georgia and the
University of New Orleans for their valuable
assistance in processing and typing information
in preparation for publication. Special recognition is expressed to Patricia Etland, University
of New Orleans, for her exceptional work in
producing the final draft of TRENDS AND ISSUES
AFFECTING CURRICULUM: PROGRAMS AND PRACTICES.

TRENDS AND ISSUES AFFECTING CURRICULUM

Educational Leadership.
ASSISTANT PRINCIPAL___, COMMUNICATION___, CON-SULTATION___, DECISION-MAKING___, DEPARTMENT HEADS___, FINANCE___, HUMANISM___, INSTRUCTION-AL LEADERSHIP___, MANAGEMENT___, ORGANIZATION___, PRINCIPALS___, SCHOOL CLIMATE___, SCHOOL BOARDS___, SUPERVISION___.

Teachers-Instruction (Pre- and In-Service Education).
ACCREDITATION___, CBTE-PBTE___, EXCHANGE TEACHERS___, FIELD EXPERIENCES___, SPECIAL SKILLS TRAINING___, STAFF DEVELOPMENT___, STUDENT TEACHING___, TEACHER CENTERS___, TEACHER EDUCATION___, TEACHER ASSESSMENT___, TEACHER EFFECTIVENESS___, TEACHING METHODS___, VIDEOTAPING___.

Teachers-Non-Instructional Aspects.
CERTIFICATION___, COLLECTIVE NEGOTIATIONS___, CONTRACTS___, COURTS/LEGAL ASPECTS___, MANAGEMENT SYSTEMS___, PROFESSIONAL ORGANIZATIONS___, TEACHER BURNOUT/STRESS___, TEACHER PERFORMANCE___, TEACHER SHORTAGE___, TEACHER'S RIGHTS___, TEXTBOOKS CONTROVERSY___.

Involvement.
COMMUNITY COLLEGE___, COMMUNITY INVOLVEMENT___, COOPERATIVE PLANNING___, DESEGREGATION___, LEGISLATION___, MULTI-CULTURAL EDUCATION___, PARENT EDUCATION___, PARENT RIGHTS/RESPON-SIBILITIES___, RESOURCES___, SCHOOL BOARDS___, SOCIAL CHANGE___, SOCIO-ECONOMIC DIFFERENCES___, TAXATION-PROPOSITION 13___.

Accountability and Evaluation.
COMPUTERIZED TESTING___, EVALUATION MODELS___, GRADING___, LEADER EVALUATION___, MASTERY LEARNING___, MINIMUM COMPETENCY TESTING___, P.L. 94-142___, PROGRAM EVALUATION___, STUDENT ACHIEVEMENT___, STUDENT COMPETENCY BASED EDUCATION___, STUDENT RIGHTS___, STUDENT/TEACHER ACCOUNTABILITY___, TESTING___.

Student Behavior.
AFFECTIVE CONCERN___, ATTENDANCE___, BEHAVIORAL
MODIFICATION___, CHILDREN OF DIVORCED___,
CONFLICT MANAGEMENT___, COOPERATION,
DELINQUENCY___, DISCIPLINE___, DROPOUT
CENTER___, DRUGS___, NUTRITION___, SCHOOL
VIOLENCE___, SELF CONCEPT___, STUDENT INTER-
ESTS___, VANDALISM___.

Curriculum Processes and Patterns.
"BACK TO BASICS" MOVEMENT___, CURRICULUM
DEVELOPMENT___, CURRICULUM REFORM/CHANGE___,
CURRICULUM OPTIONS___, FEDERAL ROLE IN
CURRICULUM___, GOALS AND PHILOSOPHY___,
OPEN EDUCATION___, PROCEDURAL OPTIONS___.

Organizational Structures.
ALTERNATIVE SCHOOLS___, EARLY CHILDHOOD
EDUCATION___, INSTRUCTIONAL MANAGEMENT
SYSTEMS___, MAGNET SCHOOLS___, MIDDLE
SCHOOLS___, SPECIAL EDUCATION PROGRAMS___,
TECHNICAL SCHOOLS___, VOCATIONAL EDUCATION___.

Curriculum Content.
AGING___, ARTS___, CAREER EDUCATION___,
COMMUNICATION SKILLS___, DEATH EDUCATION___,
ECONOMICS___, ENERGY EDUCATION___, ENVIRON-
MENTAL EDUCATION___, HEALTH AND PHYSICAL
EDUCATION___, HUMANITIES___, MATHEMATICS___,
MUSIC EDUCATION___, READING___, SCIENCE
FICTION___, SEX EDUCATION___, VALUES
EDUCATION___.

CHAPTER I
CURRICULUM BACKGROUND AND HISTORY

The curriculum of a nation's schools is a reflection of that society. If one closely studies the educational system of a nation, priorities emerge which indicate what that nation holds to be of most importance at a given point in history. By studying the background and history of American education and those civilizations which influenced it, we can better understand the forces underlying the educational emphases and the implications for curriculum content. From ancient Sparta and Athens of 2,500 years ago to our present time, we are able to analyze patterns. For example, the curriculum of ancient Sparta made it the classic example of a totalitarian society where everyone functioned as a part of the state, whereas ancient Athens developed a curriculum that is an excellent example of a comprehensive, well-balanced society. Each had its impact upon America.

Another factor which influenced the American curriculum was the Roman school, which emphasized the memorization and recitation of Latin and Greek. This was designed to produce outstanding orators who would provide leadership as Roman senators, military commanders, and governors of their far-flung empire. In later years, this emphasis on the classical subjects would be used again in the Latin grammar schools of the New England colonies.

The Middle Ages, from approximately 500 to 1500, made contributions to education through the monastic system of preserving important documents, the guild system, the emergence of German, French, Italian, and English universities, and Charlemagne's court school, which served as a model school during this period. The guild system is generally recognized as the forerunner of American vocational education and the apprenticeship system, while the early American colleges emulated the European universities.

1

When western Europe emerged from the Middle
or Dark Ages, the Renaissance and Reformation had
a great influence on the lives of the people.
Education was affected because these two movements
emphasized the importance of the individual. Later,
the sense realists, which included Comenius, Locke,
Pestalozzi, Rousseau, and Spencer, stressed the
importance of utilizing all five senses in learning.
A good example of this was the object lesson
developed by Pestalozzi, which stressed the concrete and minimized the abstract.

On looking at American educational history,
most historians agree that much of it is the
product of Western Europe. Many changes occurred
which have influenced education in America.
Probably the best technique for summarizing our
educational history is to break this history down
into time periods. For our purposes, these time
periods are Colonialism, 1600-1776; Nationalism,
1776 to 1876; Expansion and Reform, 1876 to 1929;
Increased Responsibility, 1929-1945; Hiroshima to
Sputnik, 1945-1957; Sputnik to the Moon, 1957-
1969; and Humanistic/Technological Emphases, 1970-
1980.[1]

Colonialism: 1600 to 1776

During the period of Colonialism, from 1600
to 1776, there was no central government. There
were three distinct sectional divisions: the New
England Colonies including Massachusetts, Rhode
Island, Connecticut, and New Hampshire; the Middle
Colonies including New York, New Jersey, Pennsylvania, Delaware, and Maryland; and the Southern
Colonies including Virginia, North Carolina, South
Carolina, and Georgia. Each section differed in
many ways. The New England colonies assumed a
leadership role in the colonial period. A strong
religious emphasis was prevalent as exemplified
by the Massachusetts law of 1642 which stated that

[1]William B. Ragan. Modern Elementary Curriculum,
Third Edition. New York: Holt, Rinehart, and
Winston, 1966, pp. 6-31.

parents were responsible for their children's being able to read and understand the Scriptures and the capital laws of the colonies. Since that law was difficult to enforce, it was followed by the Massachusetts law of 1647 which set the precedent for compulsory education and local control of education. This legalized taxation for education. The new law provided for a teacher when a community reached 50 families and a school building when it reached 100 families and set penalties for failure to comply. The hornbook used throughout New England was filled with religious comments and the Massachusetts law of 1647 was referred to as the "Ole Deluder Satan" Act. Other materials used were the Psalter, the Bible, and the New England Primer. In addition, the first college founded in the colonies, Harvard in 1636, was established and the graduates became teachers in the colonies. Another important contribution was the Latin grammar school founded in 1635 to prepare boys for college. The curriculum was classical in nature, with the students being required to speak, understand, and translate Greek and Latin.

The Middle Colonies made two major contributions, the academies and parochial schools. The academy was the innovation of Benjamin Franklin, who founded the first one in Philadelphia in 1751, although it was forty years later that academies became a significant factor. The academy was designed to provide a more varied and balanced curriculum than the Latin grammar school, which was the first secondary school. The academy was the second type of secondary school in America. Many of its practices have been incorporated into the modern secondary school. Both boys and girls could attend and practical subjects such as surveying, navigation, bookkeeping, and botany were offered. Parochial schools arose because of the different religious groups who settled in this area. Each group desired to maintain religious integrity. In order to insure this they established schools that preserved their religious heritage.

The Southern colonies were characterized by three different kinds of education. These were tutorial education, pauper schools, and the apprenticeship system. Tutorial education was practiced by large plantation owners who secured tutors from England and New England to instruct their sons and daughters; the products of this type of education included presidents, senators, cabinet members, and Supreme Court justices. The pauper schools were set up by religious groups from the North who sent ministers South to teach paupers, usually in a church building. Only the barest essentials of education were offered. The apprenticeship system involved indentured servants who came to the South. The master was required by law to teach his apprentice how to read, write, and use numbers. The results left much to be desired.

The three geographic regions were similar in that all established higher education institutions. Nine colleges were founded during the colonial period: Harvard (1636), William and Mary (1693), Yale (1701), Princeton (1746), King's (1754), Philadelphia (1755), Brown (1764), Queen's (1766), and Dartmouth (1769).[2] These colleges were founded by diverse religious groups including Congregationalists, Episcopalians, Presbyterians, Baptists, and others. The early colleges were strongly influenced by religious motives and provided ministers for the churches and teachers for the schools.

Nationalism: 1776 to 1876

Bridging the Colonial period and the period of Nationalism was the textbook. The textbooks utilized by the schools of a nation generally reflect the values and essential priorities of that society. Throughout early America, books emphasized what was important to the people. The

[2]James W. Hillesheim and George D. Merrill. Theory and Practice in the History of American Education. Pacific Palisades, California: Goodyear, 1971, pp. 264-265.

New England Primer, the hornbook, and the catechism were included in the curriculum of the schools in order that the early colonists could propagate their religious teachings. The test materials used in the Boston Latin Grammar School consisted primarily of Latin and Greek literature. The entrance requirements of Harvard University for the year 1643 were concerned primarily with the knowledge that a student had attained in Latin and Greek. Thus, the study of religion, Latin, and Greek held top priority for many years.

The teaching of values through textbooks continued later on in the eighteenth century when newer editions of the New England Primer began to reflect patriotic sentiments about the new nation. After the Revolution, patriotism was found in statements such as "Great Washington brave, His country did save." The New England Primer also exhorted pupils to learn their ABC's and not forever to be a blockhead.

The Primer, however, began to fade into the background after the Revolution. More appealing reading books appeared on the scene. One of the most famous was Noah Webster's "blue-backed speller," entitled Elementary Spelling Book, probably the most widely used schoolbook for the next hundred years. This book also emphasized patriotic and moralistic sentiments, making everyone who came into contact with it aware of the importance of literacy to a nation.

The period of Nationalism, from 1776 to 1876, notes the beginning of a new nation. The new states became the agencies of education. By 1800 and thereafter, the states began to set up departments of education for certification of teachers and schools and state universities after the Dartmouth Court decision in 1819 ruled against taking on private institutions for state use. During this period the school was the center of community life, and McGuffey's reader and Noah Webster's speller were the most important books. McGuffey's graded readers, published in the 1830's and 1840's, placed emphasis on achievement and success through industry, sobriety, thrift, punctuality, and other essential virtues. These readers, along with Webster's speller, set before young Americans the ideals of achievement that aided greatly in modernizing and industrializing a young country. Two important institutions, the school superintendent in 1812 and the normal school in 1839, were established. Many educators consider Horace Mann, the chief school officer in Massachusetts in the middle of the nineteenth century, the most important educator of this period. He traveled extensively in Europe and studied the practices of Pestalozzi, Herbart, and other European educators. Horace Mann was in the process of incorporating many of these innovations in the curriculum of his native state and other interested states. However, the Civil War interrupted the Common School movement and education in many sections of the country was set back a generation or two.

Two federal acts, the Northwest Ordinance of 1787 and the Morrill Act of 1862, were the first two provisions for federal aid to education. The Ordinance of 1787 set aside a one sixteenth section of each township for schools and the support of education. The Morrill Act provided for land grant colleges and universities, making it possible for students not admitted to private institutions to gain higher education. One very important court case, the Kalamazoo case, settled by the Michigan State Supreme Court in 1874, legalized the establishment and support of schools based on public taxes. This cleared the way for a tremendous growth of high schools across the country.

Another innovation during this period was the monitorial schools developed by Lancaster, in which the brightest student would teach the other students on his row. Eventually, these rows became rooms, establishing the Quincy Grammar School of Boston in 1847. This became the first graded school organization in America. The term "high school" was also first used in Boston in 1821 at the English high school.

Expansion and Reform: 1876-1929

The period of expansion and reform from 1876 to 1929 saw the beginning of provisions for individual differences through such plans as the Winnetka Plan and the Dalton Plan. Two important factors were the industrial revolution and the rise of scientific measurement. Both had profound effects on education through new means of tests and measurements and the expansion of the secondary curriculum to include grouping was promoted through the works of Thornkide, Judd, and Hall. This period saw the rise of progressive education as' expounded by John Dewey. His famous laboratory school at the University of Chicago and the later developments at Teachers College, Columbia University, are still discussed by students of education. The Committee of Ten in 1893 recommended a rigid lockstep curriculum based on the premise that all secondary students take college preparatory courses.

After the recommendations of the Committee of Ten, it was 25 years before the Commission on the Reorganization of Secondary Education responded by emphasizing the personal and social characteristics of the individual. The famous Seven Cardinal Principles (1918) exemplify the character of progressive education. These were health, command of fundamental processes, vocational efficiency, worthy home membership, citizenship, worthy use of leisure time, and ethical character. Also, Herbart helped show that learning has sequence through his five steps: preparation, presentation, association, generalization, and application. These steps aided teachers in developing unit plans and encouraged correlation of subject matter, especially in the elementary school.

Carnegie provided funds to distinguish between college and secondary work which determined that sixteen specified units would be met in the secondary school as a basis for college entrance. The Carnegie unit was designed as a measure of time which represented a year's study in one subject

area, a concept which has had a great impact on
secondary education for many years. Thus, the
Committee on College Requirements in 1899 marked
the beginning of the unit system. The Smith-
Hughes and Smith-Lever Acts a few years later set
up a federal program of vocational industrial arts
and vocational home economics for the secondary
school.

Increased Responsibility: 1929 to 1945

The period of increased responsibility from
1929 to 1945 was characterized by a growing federal
influence on education. New Deal legislation began
to have a profound effect on education. The
Federal Lunch Room Program, the Works Projects
Administration, the National Youth Administration,
the Public Works Administration, and the Civilian
Conservation Corps were examples which directly or
indirectly influenced education in the early part
of this time period. This emphasis firmly established federal aid to education,and continuing
federal programs have been a contributing factor in
curriculum programs from then until the present.
These programs provided food, materials, and
financial support for varied programs ranging from
outdoor education to professional studies.

In addition to federal programs, this was also
an era of national education committees. These
national committees conducted studies and made
recommendations to educators across the nation.
Probably the most significant curriculum study up
to this time was conducted during the period 1933
to 1941. This was the famous Eight Year Study
which cast doubt upon the idea that any single
pattern of subjects presents the best means of
preparing high school students for success in
college work. This study illustrated that many
experimental approaches are as effective as the
traditional approaches utilized in secondary schools.
It showed that students with an experimental curriculum program did as well or better in academic
college level courses than students who studied in
the traditional secondary program and excelled in

extracurricular and social activities. Thus the secondary curriculum should not be bound to any one prescribed program of studies. Elementary and junior high schools were also developing more progressive programs during this period.

The Cooperative Study of Secondary School Standards, 1933-1939, led by four regional associations, the North Central, Southern, Middle State, and Northwest, published the Evaluative Criteria in 1940 which is updated every ten years. The educators who developed the criteria emphasized that a school could be studied satisfactorily and judged fairly only in terms of its own philosophy of education, its individually expressed purposes and objectives, the nature of the pupils with whom it has to deal, the needs of the community it serves, and the nature of the American democracy of which it is a part. Thus, schools could develop and maintain individualistic programs which would be judged by comprehensive, flexible criteria rather than by narrow, uniform, and rigid guidelines. The school self-evaluation technique assists in maintaining this flexibility in evaluation.

Toward the end of this period, another national committee, Education for All American Youth, provided recommendations for the post-war United States. The Education Policies Commission was appointed by the National Education Association in 1942, and two years later they presented their report on the role of secondary schools in the years ahead. The proposed program was based on the assumption that every youth should experience a broad, balanced education whether students lived in an urban or a rural setting. This was the basis for the Ten Imperative Needs of Youth. The question arose from this committee about the role of general education as opposed to specialized education. The Harvard Report of 1945 also addressed this problem of general education for the masses. How schools can reconcile general and specialized courses so that students receive the most balanced education has been a continuing question of American educators.

Unit teaching, the project method, and adult
education were also stressed during this period,
a period that witnessed the biggest wartime operation in history and the most severe economic
depression ever recorded. Because of these
tremendous pressures, new techniques were utilized
to bring order in chaotic situations. Curriculum
techniques such as correlation, fusion, and the
broad fields approach were introduced and utilized
during this time frame. These were attempts to
synthesize great amounts of information to assist
student understanding. The continual analysis and
synthesis of information was a trait of this period
which had connotations for the next period. An
emphasis on personal and social growth, based on
practical curriculum programs, continued up to the
end of this period which ended with the conclusion
of the Second World War.

Hiroshima to Sputnik: 1945 to 1957

The period from Hiroshima to Sputnik, from
1945 to 1957, saw marked changes in the curriculum.
National committees, such as Education for All
American Youth, the Harvard Report, and others
called for a closer look at schools. A shift away
from progressive education and life adjustment was
on the increase. Non-gradedness was brought into
focus by Goodlad and Anderson. The cry for a
return to the essentials was heard across the land
and post war America slowly began to implement some
new programs. The GI Bill of 1944 assisted
8,000,000 Americans in educational benefits and
this was followed by the Korean GI Bill which also
assisted many Americans during the Fifties. Because
of the Korean War and its aftermath, both military
and civilian organizations developed programs
emphasizing American ideals. President Eisenhower
recommended a Code of Conduct for American service-
men after the "turncoat" incident of 1953. Education for All American Youth: A Further Look was a
national committee which met in 1952 to explore
these problems of political pressures, American
ideals, and loyalty. This report was presented as
a follow-up to the earlier (1944) study. The

report included recommendations dealing with an increased school population, peacetime orientation, and the felt need for fostering loyalty and citizenship education caused by the threat of communism.

The accreditation association instrument, the Evaluative Criteria, continued to exert influence over secondary and elementary schools. However, one of the most significant documents produced in this period was Bloom's Taxonomy of Educational Objectives, Handbook I: Cognitive Domain (1956), to be followed in later years by taxonomies in the affective and psychomotor domains. These taxonomies provided categories of knowledge ranging from lower to higher thinking processes by which educators could categorize educational objectives and outcomes. It was during this period that legislation was first passed providing for special education including federal and state funds for exceptional children in such areas as educable mentally retarded, trainable mentally retarded, orthopedically handicapped, and speech difficulties.

The Supreme Court decision of 1954 concerning school desegregation has had a tremendous and continuing impact on education, first in the Southern states and later across the nation. Earlier Supreme Court cases during this period included the Everson case (1947), the McCollum case (1948), and the Zorach case (1952), all of which were concerned with religion in the public schools. These cases respectively dealt with the use of public funds to pay for the bus transportation of parochial school students to their schools, the practice of "released time" instruction utilizing public school classrooms, and religious instruction being given off school property at various religious centers during regular school hours. The Supreme Court rulings on segregation and religion in the schools have provided an element of continuing controversy.

Sputnik To The Moon: 1957 to 1969

This time period witnessed the beginning of

11

the greatest era of federal aid to education. After the firing of Sputnik, the immediate response was to strengthen science, mathematics, and foreign languages. This was accomplished by the passage of the National Defense Education Act of 1958. Initially supporting science, mathematics, and foreign languages, this federal act eventually aided ten disciplinary areas. This act, along with the National Science Foundation (1950), dispensed millions of dollars to assist science and mathematics teachers. Academic year institutes, summer institutes, research fellowships, and assistance to classroom teachers in the form of audiovisual equipment and media were funded by the National Science Foundation and the National Defense Act. In an attempt to balance the support of all areas of the curriculum, the National Humanities Foundation was established in 1965.

Many other legislative acts supporting education were passed during this period, one of which created the Office of Economic Opportunity, responsible for many new programs for the disadvantaged. But the most significant federal education act was the Elementary and Secondary Education Act of 1965. This act was the first to give federal aid to all levels and areas of the curriculum. However, each program supported had to be focused on the disadvantaged. Through its many titles, it has accounted for millions of dollars to aid students classified as economically deprived. These acts provided for such well known projects as the Job Corps, the Teacher Corps, Headstart, Follow Through, Vista, and Upward Bound.

During this era many higher court decisions have affected education in such areas as integration, accountability, student rights, school financing, and religion. A pertinent example of a higher court decision affecting education was the Schempp Case (1963), in which the Supreme Court ruled on one of the most commonly found religious programs in public schools, that of Bible reading exercises. The Court held that laws providing for Bible reading violated the First Amendment and were

12

unconstitutional. In addition to this federal
legislative and judicial influence, philanthropic
foundations and industry, such as the Ford Foundation, Carnegie Foundation, and Kettering Foundation, supported educational innovations during
this period. Foundation projects covered the
spectrum of education usually as pilot programs
in selected schools with many valuable results
being passed on to schools in general. Industry
has especially influenced education through
utilization of the computer and adaptation of
industrial concepts about systems approaches,
accountability, and merit systems.

Two important studies during this period,
the Conant Report and the Trump Plan, presented
innovative ideas. The Conant Report was an
intensive study of American secondary schools
concerned with a content emphasis on "what to
teach." Many of the 21 recommendations in the
report place emphasis on students taking more
subjects per school day with much enrichment. The
Trump Plan was concerned with "how to teach" and
is organized around three types of instruction:
large group instruction, small group instruction,
and independent study. These three types of
instruction formed the basis for Trump's team
teaching plan. Team teaching is a systematic
arrangement wherein several teachers with a leader
and assistants, and with optimum use of technology,
cooperatively instruct a group of students by
making the best use of the competencies of each
member of the teaching team. In addition to these
two studies, Jerome Bruner's Process of Education
outlined for education the structure of knowledge
and how it could be applied at all educational
levels. This was followed by mastery learning
spearheaded by Benjamin Bloom. The individualization of instruction has been a key factor in
curriculum design through projects such as Individually Prescribed Instruction (IPI) with the
emphasis on individual development and growth.

This period drew to a close at the end of the

13

Sixties when the United States, in a tremendous 12 year effort, placed men on the moon. This feat culminated a period of rapid change and world restlessness, especially in Third World Nations. While great technological feats were being accomplished, many parts of the world were still living in varying degrees of poverty. Thus, the stage was set for the Seventies involving the problem of combining the best features of technology and humanism.

Humanistic/Technological Emphases: 1970 to 1980

The decade of the seventies has been characterized by both humanistic and technological advances. Beginning in the early part of the decade, career education and reading were emphasized with many of these programs being initiated at the U.S. Office of Education. A continuing interest in behavioral objectives and behavior modification was maintained at the beginning of the decade. In the humanistic areas, the seventies witnessed a concerted effort to protect the rights of the individual through legal or other means. Movements in multicultural education, women's rights, draft counseling, values clarification, and moral education appeared on the scene with emotional responses from various groups representing the entire political spectrum. This produced a climate conducive for censorship of textbooks and curriculum materials. These heated confrontations occurred in different sections of the nation and were typical of the strong feelings aroused when the cognitive and affective domain overlap. In addition to these movements, a continuing effort to assist exceptional children has been strengthened and many new programs have been implemented.

The seventies have also been marked by a growing number of lobbyists at both the federal and state levels representing certain programs or educational organizations. Teachers have become more organized and a concurrent event has been the increased emphasis on staff development programs for all teachers. Thus, both the individual and the organized group have received additional support during the 1970's possibly as a reaction to the stunning blows of Vietnam, Watergate, and the energy crunch. These events left many Americans searching for guidelines and ideals which seemed to be lost. Recovery from national problems are time consuming and extract a toll on those involved in education.

The increasing use of technological developments in schools such as cable television, closed-circuit television, teaching machines, computers, and dial access retrieval systems insures that education will never be the same. Major forces influencing the curriculum include the decline in national test scores, public concern for career orientation of school graduates, student apathy, and an increased emphasis on the modes of inquiry in curriculum improvement projects fostered through Research and Development centers. National assessment studies and national secondary reform proposals in the early seventies provided many recommendations for modified education. Reports from these projects are exemplified by Youth: Transition to Adulthood, Continuity and Discontinuity, and American Youth in the Seventies. Other factors affecting the curriculum during this period include increased federal aid to education, an increased emphasis on "back to the basics," concern for stereotyping in textbooks and other educational materials, and an increased emphasis on educational accountability at all levels. Again, higher court cases have been affecting education with the recent emphasis on equality of education and school financing in landmark cases in Texas and California. Viewing these many forces affecting the curriculum and the implications for the schools, one must conclude that this last period in educational history has been one of much activity and a shifting of emphases on various aspects of the school curriculum.

In summary, the developing and continuous nature of the curriculum has been traced through various time periods until the present. Even now, curricular changes are occurring which will have varying degrees of impact. By understanding the political, sociological, and educational developments of our nation in relation to the development of curriculum during the time periods discussed in this chapter, students can better apply examples from history in working with current educational issues, problems, and trends.

CHAPTER II
EDUCATIONAL LEADERSHIP

The challenging need of every school system
is that of a comprehensive concept of education
which is understood, fostered, and supported by
administrators, teachers, and boards of education.
This concept encompasses education for all persons
according to their specific personal needs and
interests. Development and implementation of such
an education depends upon educational leadership
which is no longer confined to administrators.
Classroom teacher groups and a wide variety of
organizations are demanding and getting participation in decision-making and goal setting.
Parents, motivated by the new thrust for all
citizen involvement, are exercising their right
to determine and control their children's education.

Classroom teachers are making decisions that
were formerly made by administrators and supervisors and are serving more in the role of coordinators of various learning activities and
experiences. The teachers of today are a diverse
group with a broad range of specialities whose
actions are dictated more by societal conditions
than by administrative edict. Curriculum development and instructional procedures are being
influenced by educational organizations and by
inservice education and decision-making processes
organized according to subject areas with specialists in these areas taking the lead.

Students are increasingly more vocal and
willing to confront the educator and are getting
attention. However, they do recognize and respond
to leadership which takes them into consideration.
Interaction with students to prevent and relieve
conflict and frustration is a major responsibility
and function of educational leadership.

Educators are increasingly confronted by
demands that they be more accountable for the

learning successes or failures of students. Student performance is increasingly being linked with teacher performance, and the administration is required to develop and implement systematic teacher evaluation systems. This entails the setting of goals delineated through educational objectives which can and are being consistently evaluated. Much of this pressure comes from groups outside recognized educational circles who have pressed for accountability in student achievement. Along side this academic accountability thrust is a substantive body of research supporting the humanistic approach. It shows that student involvement and identification with school are essential in students' growth and development.

Many traditional methods and devices in education are causing students to raise serious questions about education's relevance to the real world and causing them to lose confidence in "the establishment." Efforts by the public to make educators more accountable have, in many situations, only magnified the cognitive learning overload for students. Programmed sets of objectives prescribed for classroom use provide a poor climate for understanding and limited circumstances for application by the learner. On the other hand, conditions for learning are improved when students are given opportunities to raise questions, to be confronted with inconsistencies, and are permitted to sort out appropriate values at their own pace. In such a humanistic climate, teachers and administrators have better rapport with each other, and student discipline problems are diminished.

Many steps are being taken to cope with contemporary problems of concern to educational leaders on more understandable terms. Realizing that communication is paramount to an educator, effort has been made to improve this skill among administrators. Workshops for this purpose have proven to be effective. Involvement of a broader scope of persons in decision-making is not only improving communication, it is tapping new resources and gaining support toward meeting educational goals. Examples can be found which include student councils, faculty councils, and parent councils. The extreme format for increasing involvement may be found where one state legislature mandated that each school system have an advisory committee. The most effective participation seems to come when administrators voluntarily take the initiative in providing opportunities for a spectrum of persons to function in a school system's decision-making process.

Possibly the strongest factor in the shift of the leadership role of the principal has been the desegregation movement. The mixing of ethnic groups has changed the role, emphasis, and function of school administrators. Persons in these positions have been forced to exert new skills in leadership, organization, and facilitation. Court-mandated shifts of students and teachers into situations for which educators were ill prepared have changed the entire educational climate in numerous situations. The problems encountered and the magnified need for better paid and more different kinds of personnel and instructional media are just being recognized and given some attention and support.

It is being recognized more positively that educators, teachers or administrators, cannot be expected to emerge from their initial college preparation program with knowledge and skills required to function continuously in their chosen areas of speciality. Continuous and comprehensive assistance with development of new skills and knowledge are necessitated by our changing society. The burden of this on-going responsibility for professional growth lies with educational leadership. However, time and preparation are not adequate for administrators to personally perform this function, therefore special assistance is provided in a variety of staff positions. Department heads provide the first line of support, but these persons are also inadequately prepared and

19

frequently without time to perform this important role. Consequently, supervisory persons with special expertise in curriculum and instruction are employed to assume primary responsibility for assisting all professional personnel in keeping up and in making education more effective for the learner.

Inservice education and/or staff development under the leadership of supervisors is being recognized as a necessary function in most school systems. In larger systems a collaboration of a variety of specialists and resource persons provide the major source of continuing staff development. Consultants and outside specialists from neighboring systems, State departments of education, institutions of higher education, and regional educational service agencies provide sporadic technical consultative assistance. Curriculum supervisors provide the major leadership in curriculum development on a systemwide basis in some large school systems.

There continues to be indecision as to the role and function of supervisors. Findings from a national committee recognized that what supervisors are expected to do varies according to the position they hold and the districts in which they work. This is aggravated by conflict between teachers and administrators. Teachers want direct assistance from supervisors, while administrators place them in roles such as preparation of proposals for federal grants and evaluation of teachers. One national committee agreed that there should be two distinct supervisory positions identified as (1) administrative instructional supervisors and (2) consultative instructional supervisors with different preparation and certification for each.

Studies have shown that principals, like most professionals, give more attention to that with which they feel most comfortable and for which they have been best prepared and that which they perceive their systemwide superiors to give major priority. Consequently, the development of curriculum and

20

supervision of instruction receive limited attention from administrators. There are some situations, however, where the school has been turned from an era of chaos to one of educational effectiveness by a principal. Examples of such schools and research findings indicate that these developments usually come when there is a principal who gives priority to instructional leadership, is able to deal with goal setting and goal communication, has an understanding of youth, and an ability to share leadership with others. Some research, however, in regard to what influence administrators have on instruction, has shown that administrative features and environmental pressures have little effect on classroom instruction. This research points out that a better chance for improving instruction seems to be possible when the principal follows a supervisory model and makes provision for peer observation. Such a model usually provides for agreeing on expected outcomes, sharing information, and working toward improvement in light of findings.

A factor of increasing concern is the amount of political pressure encountered by school board members, administrators, and legislators. Such is increasingly influencing support for education, much of the educational process, and some curriculum content. This gives strong argument for utilization of some kind of systematic management system. Management by Objectives (MBO) has been tried unsuccessfully in a number of school systems but is being used successfully in many others. The major advantage of this system is the necessity of formulating objectives in keeping with needs of a particular school system and providing for these needs according to a plan. Another system called pro-management is now being proclaimed by some school systems. This is an approach to employee relations which keeps administrators and teachers communicating and working toward common objectives. Without the guidance of definite goals and objectives and a plan of operation, pressure groups can very easily

cause educators to lose sight of their main
purpose for being.

Changing societal and educational conditions
indicate that educational leadership is increasingly becoming a shared responsibility. It is continuously assessing needs of students and society
and adjusting curriculum accordingly. Decisions
being made by educational leadership are the major
force in improving or retarding educational
effectiveness. Persons in these positions are
called upon continuously to interpret educational,
political, and societal concerns in terms of
educational effectiveness. The principal is the
key to leadership in a humanistic open approach
to education. Communication and all-level-persons
involvement are receiving increased attention.
Shared leadership plans are involving teachers
more directly in decision-making and in curriculum
development and implementation. Management systems
are being used to determine and implement educational objectives and to maintain effective
personnel relations. Supervisory personnel
function as members of an instructional team
providing expertise in curriculum and instruction.

SYNOPSES

THE BOSTON STORY: MEETING THE CHALLENGE OF
   DESEGREGATION

Alson, Allan and Charles H. Gibbons, Jr. National
   Elementary Principal, Volume 58, March 1979,
   pp. 62-66.

        Alson and Gibbons report some changes in the
role and function of principals brought about by
desegregation of Boston schools. The Federal
Court Desegregation Decision there required that
individual school plans be completed by all city
principals. Principals were expected to exert
educational leadership as well as continue being
organizational managers and facilitators. An
example of what took place may be seen in the
Tobin Elementary School. There the principal,
staff, and parents cooperatively set clear organizational and educational priorities to carry out
desegregation. Before attending to curriculum,
staff development, or formal parent involvement,
two tasks had to be met. These priorities were
1) to convince white parents their children would
be safe to and from school and while in this
black housing project area, and 2) to establish
a quality educational program for those children
being transferred to this school.

        The authors report that the challenge did
not end when students were transported safely to
school. The principal launched a three pronged
attack on curriculum development, staff development, and parent participation. As the first
step a council was established to accommodate
parents' needs and a teacher coordinator was
appointed to serve as facilitator and resource
person to the parent council. Spanish and English
classes were offered for parents who did not speak
either of the languages. Other basic curriculum
endeavors were carried out, and a fine arts
program including drama and music was established.
Boston University, the paired institution required

23

by the courts, contributed significantly to curriculum and staff development.

Through the principal's efforts, and with the cooperation of parents and staff, the students attending this school were safe, involved in worthwhile programs, and their parents were a part of the process. The authors view the principal's role as responsible for these results and feel it can be replicated by other principals who are willing to try. It is a striking example of what was done by one school principal to carry out in good faith the order of the courts in regard to desegregation.

HERE'S HOW THREE SCHOOL SYSTEMS MAKE PRO-MANAGE-MENT WORK

Anderson, Bill. The American School Board Journal. Volume 166, March 1980, pp. 22, 23, 42.

Anderson tells how pro-management is working in three school systems. He says this is a means of keeping employees happy by making it easy for them to deal directly with the board and administration without a union. Two schools in Texas and one in California have avoided recognizing a teacher union for purposes of bargaining.

According to Anderson, the Dallas Independent School District has a carefully laid plan under the direction of a deputy superintendent in charge of employee relations. That plan includes professional ombudsmen, operation involvement-faculty committees on budgetary and instructional policy, and a district communication committee.

The systems five full-time ombudsmen handle teacher complaints - whatever they are. Whereas systems the size of Dallas have 100 to 200 formal grievances filed by teachers each year, Dallas has had only ten in the last two years. Each school faculty elects a representative (with release time) to each of the school system's 24 faculty committees. These committees draw up specific proposals relating to school policy to be presented to the school board. The communications committee works on salary and benefit packages for all employees.

The Pasadena (Texas) Independent School District emphasizes two-way communication between teachers and administrators. It has a communications committee composed of one representative for every 25 of the system's 2,000 teachers. These representatives meet in groups to discuss all kinds of teacher proposals. Recommendations from these groups are prepared by small committees as formal proposals for the administrations' consideration. These are submitted to the superintendent's spokesman who serves as an intermediary between the teachers and administration. A needs assessment conducted once or twice each year by the faculty representative at each school gives teachers the opportunity to express the ten most important changes they would like to see in the schools.

Anderson says the chief tool of communication in the Clovis Unified School District, near Fresno, California is the Faculty Senate, a group of teachers representing all 16 of the system's schools. The administration of the school system has made clear its views about unions, fought for what is thought best for the schools, and made it possible through the representative approach for teachers to have a say in virtually all school matters. Teachers are encouraged to go directly to their principals, and principals have a large share of autonomy in their own schools. The school board sets common goals but the individual schools are free to approach these goals in their own ways.

Anderson suggests that even though a school system may be unionized, it might try some of the pro-management tactics these school systems use. He says this approach to keeping employees happy is nothing more than a new name for sound management.

25

IMPROVING COMMUNICATION SKILLS OF ADMINISTRATORS

Beale, Andrew V. and William A. Bost. NASSP
    Bulletin, Volume 63, April 1979, pp. 31-39.

Beale and Bost share information about their
efforts to determine if emphatic communication
skills of school administrators can be improved
through use of a workshop in a metropolitan
school system. Convinced that the human element
of communication is critical in school administration, they conducted a workshop for assistant principals from twenty-six schools as a
part of the principals' regular inservice training
program.

The short-term, didactic-experimental workshop designed to influence emphatic discrimination
abilities of participants included lecture, role-
playing, and large and small group discussion
organized according to Gordon's Human Effectiveness Training Model. Specific attention was
given to enabling the administrators to discern
the appropriateness of using certain categories
of verbal responses. The workshop gave assistance
in dealing with road blocks to communication,
behavior found unacceptable, confronting without
hurting, problem solving, and values conflicts.
Response classifications considered were evaluative
(commander-in-chief), instructive (know it all),
placating (the consoler), probing (the interrogator)
and understanding (leveler).

An instrument called the Administrator
Empathy Discrimination Index (AEDI), constructed
to determine the effectiveness of the workshop,
was used as pre- and post-test. It is a forced-
choice instrument requiring the rating of
situations relevant to the categories of verbal
responses on a five point scale. The categories
are the same as those taught in the workshop.

According to Beal and Bost, scores noting
the difference between pre- and post-tests were
determined and empathy discrimination ability

26

was monitored using the Wilcox Matched Pairs
Signed Ranks Test. The pre-test revealed an
emphasis on the probing or "helping" response.
The post-test indicated this had been reduced
by one-half but still remained heavy. Comparison
of the beginning and end scores for the participants in the workshop showed a reduction in
probing responses and an increase in understanding
responses. Although the authors recognized need
for further study, they concluded that communi-
cative skills can be enhanced through active
participation in a relatively short-term training
program. Such a program can enhance the ability
to communicate empathetically with others, a
vitally needed skill in working with people.

HOW MUCH INFLUENCE DO (AND CAN) EDUCATIONAL
    ADMINISTRATORS HAVE ON CLASSROOMS?

Deal, Terrence E. and Lynn D. Celotti. Phi
    Delta Kappan, Volume 61, March 1980,
    pp. 471-473.

        Research conducted by Deal and Celotti reveals
a picture of the relationship between classroom
instruction and school organization different to
that generally expected. A three-year study was
conducted with thirty-four school districts in
the San Francisco Bay (California) area. Data
were analyzed to determine how roles, policies,
and administrative practices at school and district
level affected classroom organization and instruction. Particular attention was given to individualized instruction and team teaching, assuming
that the two would be related, would be affected
by district or school organizational or administrative patterns, and by characteristics of the
community environment.

        Superintendents and principals of 103
elementary schools (selected randomly for the
study) were interviewed and completed short
questionnaires, as a pre-test in 1973 and as a
post-test in 1975. Teachers in 18 of the schools

responded in a similar design. Administrators and teachers were asked to describe instructional and organizational patterns from their respective viewpoints.

Findings of the study showed that higher levels of individualized classroom instruction between 1973 and 1975 were fostered by open space architecture and California's specially funded Early Childhood Education program. Individualized instruction, however, was not affected by the organization of the classroom or by organization or administrative features of the school. Important aspects of classroom instruction were similarly unaffected by district-level character-istics or the leadership style of the superinten-dent. With the exception of the effects of California's Early Childhood program, classroom instruction, with reference to materials variation, student grouping, or pacing, appears to be independent of environmental pressures. It was noted that in districts where teachers' organi-zations were reported as highly influential that close-working relationships, reference team teaching, actually declined between 1973 and 1975. Open space, however, did have a positive effect on the organization of the classroom. The authors concluded, therefore, that the classroom is a relatively autonomous unit with its instructional or organizational characteristics shielded from formal influence by the community, district office, principal or the teacher next door.

Based on these findings, Deal and Celotti suggest several implications for administrators. According to the authors, administrative action in regard to instruction might well be centered on areas other than organization, such as credentialing, discipline, curriculum topics, and by using more informal strategies in working with teachers. They suggest that as senior colleagues or symbolic leaders, administrators may be able to have a positive effect on classroom instruction.

CUSTODIAL HIGH SCHOOLS AND SELF ACTUALIZATION OF
   STUDENTS

Deibert, John P. and Wayne K. Hoy. Educational
   Research Quarterly, Volume 2, Summer 1977,
   pp. 24-36.

     In a study done by Deibert and Hoy in New
Jersey, it was found that high school students
who attend a custodial high school are less
inner directed, time competent, and self actualized
than students who attend humanistic high schools.
The humanistic oriented school was identified as
an educational community in which students learn
through cooperative interaction and experience.
The custodial oriented school referred to the
traditional school with a rigid and highly
controlled setting concerned primarily with the
maintenance of order. Three hypotheses were
tested: 1) the more custodial the pupil control
orientation of a high school the less self-
actualized the pupil, 2) the more custodial the
pupil control orientation of a high school the
less inner directed the students, and 3) the more
custodial the pupil control orientation of a
high school the less time competent the students.

     The authors report that data were collected
on site from 6,000 teachers and students in
forty high schools in New Jersey that were
representative in terms of size of school and
equalized valuation per pupil of the communities
from which the pupils came. The Pupil Control
Ideology (PCI) was administered to teachers and
the Pupil Orientation Inventory (POI) was
administered to sophomore and senior pupils in
each school. Since the unit of analysis in this
study was the school organization, the information
obtained from respondents was pooled to reflect
the properties of the school. The PCI data
yielded information about custodialism of the
school while the POI data reflected the self-
actualization scores of the student body in each
school.

Testing the hypotheses using correlation
analysis, Deibert and Hoy found that the more
custodial the school, the less likely the students
were basically inner directed and time competent.
They also concluded that girls achieved a significantly higher level of self-actualization
than boys and that size of school was typically
not related to student body self-actualization
with one exception - the larger the school, the
less the time-competence of students. On the
other hand, the study showed that the wealthier
the school district, the greater the tendency
of students to be inner directed, time-competent,
and self-actualized.

Conclusions drawn from the study by Deibert
and Hoy were that the control orientation of
schools does have an impact on the development
of personalities in young people; and that the
more humanistic (less custodial) the pupil
control orientation of a school, the greater the
chance that high school students are moving
toward self-actualization in the sense that they
are learning to experience their own potential
in a meaningful way. According to the authors,
the school needs to provide leadership which will
assist the student to work out solutions to
problems for himself in his own way.

PEER OBSERVATION: A MEANS FOR SUPERVISORY
    ACCEPTANCE

Ellis, Elmer C., Joseph T. Smith, and William
    Harold Abbott, Jr. Educational Leadership,
    Volume 36, March 1979, pp. 423-426.

An elementary principals' success with
clinical supervision/peer observation is described
by Ellis, Smith, and Abbott. The program designed
and carried out by the principal and teachers in
the Bailey Elementary School of Tifton, Georgia
employed a pre-test, use of a clinical supervision
cycle with peer observation teams, and post-test.

According to the authors, an attitude scale, designed and field tested by the principal, was administered to all teachers in the school on the first day of the 1976-77 preplanning session. Following this, a scheme to change teacher perceptions of supervision was implemented. Under the leadership of a committee of three teachers and the principal, an observation program was designed.

The committee selected Cogan's clinical supervision cycle as the process for peer observation and Flander's Interaction Analysis and the Georgia Revision of the Purdue Observation Instrument for use during the observation cycle. The principal and two school system central staff persons provided training in use of the instruments. Needs of individual teachers were identified and peer observation teams were formed.

Ellis and his associates report that the principal completed the first round of clinical observations giving feedback to teachers and familiarizing them with the clinical cycle in actual practice. Each member of the peer observation teams visited each other twice, and the principal completed his clinical observations after which the pre-test attitude scale was administered as a post-test.

According to the authors, analysis of statistical data from the various tests showed that the attitudes of teachers in the school toward supervision had improved significantly. The conclusions are that teachers feel more at ease when someone is observing them, they are more inclined toward asking assistance from others, and the purposes of supervision are better understood. The authors further conclude that "teachers are more receptive to supervision: when they have helped to determine its purposes and procedures; when the supervision is for the purpose of assisting them to do a better job and not for evaluation; and, when the problems being worked on are, indeed, the teacher's problems as he/she perceives them."

ADVISORY COMMITTEES - DOES ANYBODY WANT THEIR ADVICE?

Fisher, Allen. Educational Leadership, Volume 37, December 1979, pp. 254-255.

Fisher reports the dilemma faced when the Florida Legislature ordered the state's 67 county schools to establish advisory committees representative of their communities. To determine the results of this action, Fisher conducted a survey of 140 advisory committee members serving various levels of administration in the seven largest county districts. Realizing that increasing effort is being directed toward bringing more people into the decision-making process, he wanted to see to what extent such persons were actually "bridging the gap between educators and members of the public that pay the bills" as this Florida legislative directive proposed.

In an examination of the education levels of the committee persons, Fisher found that the amount of formal schooling of the advisory members was sufficient for them to offer advice to educators. Nevertheless, responses by these persons indicated that their effective influence with school authorities was severely limited and in some cases non-existent. Involvement of advisory members in helping generate financial support was disappointingly low. Assistance in the evaluation of teachers and administrators was completely barred from advisory committees. Little of significance could be cited where advisory members were able to participate in school affairs, and in some instances they reported being treated with complete indifference. However, there were some examples of successful advisory group action.

Fisher notes that the blame for lack of

involvement was not fully on educators. Many members reported that school authorities were open for suggestions, but the advisory persons lacked the particular knowledge and experience for effective participation. This points to the fact that failure was built into the system - the delegation to local authorities of almost total discretion over the duties and authority of these committees. Without definition of power and delineation of responsibilities,too many followed the old line of leaving education to the professionals. The committees,having been imposed from outside the educational system,consequently created prejudice and misunderstanding, the very things it had been anticipated they would improve.

Fisher suggests that in this time of tightening resources, declining enrollments, and growing resentment of overall public services, educators would do well to make an extra effort to use advisory groups of whatever nature to the maximum. Educators should take the initiative in seeking involvement from the public rather than wait for the public to call upon them.

IF YOU FOLLOW THESE PROVEN GUIDELINES, MERIT PAY FOR ADMINISTRATORS CAN SUCCEED

Geiger, Philip E. and Gerald Toscano. The American School Board Journal, Volume 166, January 1980, pp. 31-33.

In an effort to develop a management by objectives (MBO) - based merit pay plan for Galloway Township, New Jersey, Geiger and Toscano reviewed merit pay plans introduced in a number of school systems. From this study they report factors common to the most successful merit pay plans, factors common to unsuccessful plans. and a brief review of several merit pay plans implemented in school systems around the United States.

Some factors found to be common to the most

33

successful plans were 1) the superintendent
appointed a committee of administrators to draw
up plans, 2) the superintendent took the initiative
in gaining school board support, 3) all administrators participated, 4) administrators helped
set performance objectives for themselves, 5) a
high percentage of each administrator's salary
was earned on merit, and 6) the numerical cut-
off point for receiving merit pay was known only
to the superintendent. Some factors common to
unsuccessful plans included use of merit pay by
the superintendent for political purposes or
manipulation, goals and objectives not designed
for individuals, and the plans made no provision
for rewarding imagination and creativity.

Merit pay plans reported by Geiger and Toscano
as continuing to function are Forest Hills School
District, Cincinnati; Northern Valley Regional
Schools, Closter, New Jersey; Topeka (Kansas)
Unified School District No. 501; and Madison
(Wisconsin) Public Schools. Varying degrees of
success were cited.

The superintendent of the Forest Hills Schools
spoke with pride and confidence of his two-year-
old program which he says provided involvement
from the people directly affected through an
administrative council. Superintendent Howarth
of Northern Valley Regional Schools says the
school board and administrators are supportive
of their plan which bases pay on numerical rating
related to job description and job target. The
Topeka School District plan, in operation for
five years, determines merit increased by a
numerical score from the immediate supervisor of
each administrator submitted to the superintendent's
council (twelve top administrators) for final
determination of increases. Superintendent Rickie
credits the survival of Madison Schools merit pay
program to the function of a panel of administrators
with representation from every level of administration.

The authors cite three school systems that

34

tried a merit pay program which has ceased to function. Superintendent Zieman found the Appleton (Wisconsin) Area School District plan too expensive. The fact that administrative pay was tied to teacher raises put principals in the position of boosting teacher salaries in the interest of the principal's salary. According to Superintendent Pigg, the merit pay plan of Dubuque (Iowa) Community School District focused attention on who got how many points rather than school function and was eventually voted down by the principals. The Chicago Public Schools merit pay system was dropped after two years operation because evaluations of administrators immediately improved to the point of necessitating more money than was available.

The study by Superintendent Geiger and elementary principal Toscano provided evidence sufficient for them to recommend that an M.B.O.-based merit pay plan be designed for the administrative team of the Galloway Township School System. Examples of successful and not so successful experiences of school systems with merit pay have been provided for the consideration of others.

THE ROLE OF THE PRINCIPAL IN COMMUNITY INVOLVEMENT

Hines, Susan C. and Lloyd E. McCleary. NASSP
    Bulletin, Volume 64, January 1980, pp. 67-75.

Hines and McCleary report findings from a study to determine the orientation of high school principals to their role in community involvement. This study was made as part of the effort of the Rockefeller Family Fund and the National Association of Secondary School Principals (NASSP) to assist high school principals.

Principals identified as effective by the 1977-78 NASSP National High School Principalship Study were used to survey belief patterns of effective principals in regard to community involvement. These principals were asked to rate the level of citizen/parent concern in several areas.

The study revealed, according to Hines and McCleary, that principals saw the number one concern expressed by parents as that of "use of drugs/dope" with "lack of discipline" as the number two problem in schools. They reported that the next concerns of parents in order of importance were drinking/alcoholism; crime/vandalism; and lack of financial support. In response to the inquiry as to the negative impact of the same problem areas in the next four years, the principals identified "lack of financial support," "collective bargaining by teachers," "use of drugs/dope/alcohol," and "declining enrollments" as areas of highest impact.

Principals reported communication was initiated by parents most by telephone. This reflects the view that one-to-one verbal communication is the most important means of communicating with parents. Printed/written matter in order to confirm, reinforce, and develop a consistent record was rated as next in importance. Major areas identified by principals as requiring the attention of citizens are 1) economic conditions, including teacher demands; 2) accountability and setting of priorities and objectives; 3) school programs; and 4) legal/judicial actions.

The authors conclude that high school principals recognize the importance of community involvement and have little option as to participation. They are seeking to establish and maintain two-way communication with the community through planned and informal procedures on a continuing basis. Specific findings from the Rockefeller/NASSP study provide a data bank which can be helpful to principals.

THE UNTOLD GOLDEN STATE STORY: AFTERMATH OF
    PROPOSITION 13

Hoban, Gary. Phi Delta Kappan, Volume 61,
    September 1979, pp. 18-21.

Hoban reports on the aftermath of Proposition

13 in California and its impact upon public education in that state. Much confusion surrounds Proposition 13, but Hoban points out that certain areas are already hurting such as abolition of summer school, the termination notices to 28,809 teachers although there was considerable attrition without replacement leaving about 11,000 dismissed, low morale, and pupil welfare services. His study reveals a decline in total number of personnel in four categories: administration; pupil services, including librarians, nurses, and counselors; classroom teachers; and classified support personnel.

In general, instructional programs seemed to suffer less than personnel as a result of Proposition 13. Districts that made substantial reductions in staff usually continued most classroom programs with minor reductions. According to Hoban, the most severely affected area was that of pupil welfare services, and to a lesser degree, special education.

Perhaps the most significant aftermath of Proposition 13 for educators has been low morale since 1978. Although morale is difficult to define, a general sense of frustration and disillusion has been noted by many observers. California has not had time yet to assess the results of its tax revolt, but Hoban points out that two initiatives are facing the state in 1980: the "Spirit of 13" initiative for limits on government spending and the Robbins antibusing initiative. Decisions of the voters will determine the quality of education in California.

A BASIS FOR IMPROVED INSTRUCTIONAL LEADERSHIP

Niedermeyer, Fred C. The Elementary School Journal, Volume 77, January 1977, pp. 248-254.

Niedermeyer describes an instructional leadership model which was tested by the South West Regional Laboratory (SWRL) of Los Alomitos,

California. The model consists of the following sequential steps: 1) agreeing on achievement outcomes and standards, 2) sharing information on achievement, and 3) working to improve instruction in the light of identified learning deficiencies. The program used for testing the model was the SWRL Beginning Reading Program. Special resource materials for instructional supervision were developed to accompany the program.

The reading program provided for administrators working with teachers in agreeing upon indicators of class achievement such as an acceptable minimum score for pupils on each unit tested. It further provided that when problems of substandard class achievement were identified, the teacher and administrator would examine the teacher's instructional activities and formulate modification. A simple convenient information system was used to record class performance by which the teacher and administrator could quickly determine if there was an instructional problem. The SWRL program specified a variety of resources and procedures for assisting teachers in responding to class achievement or rate of completion according to goals.

The supervision resource materials were tested in varying patterns, according to the supervision model, in ninety-nine kindergarten classes of thirty-six elementary schools from eight districts.

Twenty-four of the thirty-six schools were randomly selected to use the supervision resource materials with the reading program. The other twelve served as comparison schools. At the end of the school year all classes were post-tested.

According to Niedermeyer, the data showed that in schools where resources for supervision were used, students had a higher rate of program completion (80 percent) than in comparison schools (60 percent). Negative teacher reaction to the instructional supervision procedures was expressed at only one of the twenty-four experimental schools.

He therefore concluded that the instructional
supervision models can improve pupils' achievement
in an outcomes-based, classroom-verified instructional program.

WINGATE: BROOKLYN'S BORN-AGAIN HIGH SCHOOL

Savage, David G. Educational Leadership, Volume
    36, May 1979, pp. 541-544.

David Savage describes how principal Robert
Schain cut through administrative trivia, tackled
reading and the rest of the curriculum, and turned
George Wingate High School in Brooklyn, New York
into a "model of urban education."

In the early 1970's Wingate was chaotic, a
"rathole" with nearly all black and mostly poor
students reading two grades below grade-level,
said Principal Schain. The students had no
interest in education, and the mostly white
faculty was demoralized and frightened.

Savage reported in 1978 that the school was
neat, halls orderly, lawns well-kept, and bath-
rooms were used for intended purposes rather than
as a center of drug traffic. The halls were not
patrolled by security officers, the students
seemed interested in getting an education, and
eighty percent were going on to higher education.

According to the author, Schain admits to
having no grand plan to turn Wingate around. He
saw a two-fold interrelated problem when he first
came to Wingate: a school where disruption won
out over education and where most of the students
could barely read.

Recognizing reading as basic to learning,
Schain began an intensive basic skills mini-school
with his best, young dedicated teachers working
closely with the poorest students. An intensive
English program was developed for the influx of
French speaking students from Haiti. Both programs

paid dividends. As students began to learn and make progress and realize that teachers cared about them, disruption began to decline.

The teachers of all subject areas began to incorporate reading into their curriculum. A handbook, "Developing Reading Skills Through Subject Areas," was written, edited, designed, and printed at Wingate. Funds gained from the sale of the book were used to purchase needed educational materials.

Wingate also provided alternative courses in the curriculum to interest the students. Some of the new courses included psychology in literature, sports literature, Greek mythology, modern dance, photography, and anthropology. Specialized institutes developed were: flight training, legal procedures, international relations, and medical science. In these institutes students get "hands on" experiences working part-time in appropriate locations.

The author says Schain is first and foremost a teacher who spends almost no time talking about discipline and administrative trivia. He manages to keep a sense of humor. Possibly his strongest trait is the ability to involve others in the decision-making process and to enable teachers to create new ideas and giving them the support necessary for succesful development. These traits are partially responsible for the "Born-Again" Wingate.

INSTRUCTIONAL SUPERVISORS: A DICHOTOMY

Sturgis, A. W. Educational Leadership, Volume 36, May 1979, pp. 586-589.

Sturgis reviews the efforts of an Association for Supervision and Curriculum Development (ASCD) working group to define the roles of instructional supervisors and reports some conclusions of the group. He reports that the group reviewed more than 100 research reports, texts, articles, standards of regional accrediting agencies, current certification requirements, and views of members from professional organizations representing those who prepare, employ, and work with instructional supervisors. The group sought to determine 1) the purposes of instructional supervision, 2) the roles and responsibilities of supervisors, and 3) the activities of supervisors.

The study did not reveal a definitive role description for instructional supervisors. It found what supervisors are expected to do varies according to the position they hold and the district in which they work. Sturgis views what he describes as a conflict: teachers want direct assistance in improving learning opportunities of children, but they see supervisors in administrative roles not directly related to improving instruction. Writers about supervision seem to agree that supervision is a process intended to improve learning opportunities for students.

The basic conclusion drawn by the ASCD group is that supervision, according to the roles they were able to establish, encompasses two positions which are 1) administrative instructional supervisor and 2) consultative instructional supervisor. Delineation of the two positions placed responsibilities of administrative supervisors as that of such tasks as preparation of proposals of federal grants and evaluation of teachers for tenure and salary increase. Responsibilities of consultative supervisors were described as those more directly involved with helping teachers improve methodology and evaluation of teachers to improve performance from a diagnostic point of view aimed at helping them improve the learning opportunities of children.

Sturgis summarized by deeming it appropriate to have two separate positions for persons who would have different academic preparations and hold different titled certificates. It was agreed

that both would have teaching experience and
that clinical supervision would be a part of
their preparation programs. This distinction
between the two roles at the school system level
could enhance the success potential of both types
of supervisor.

CAN PRINCIPALS LEAD IN CURRICULUM DEVELOPMENT?

Vann, Allan. Educational Leadership, Volume 36,
    March 1979, pp. 404-405.

    A study by Allan Vann shows that principals
give emphasis to the areas for which they are
adequately trained and their perceptions of what
their central office superiors consider important.
The study involved 50 principals in a suburban
county of New York.

    From a review of major studies of the elemen-
tary school principalship, Vann concluded that
many principals neglect their responsibilities
as leaders in curriculum development. Finding
also that the studies indicated these same
persons indicated they would prefer to devote
more time to curriculum development, he sought
to determine what prevented them from doing so.

    Vann found that where principals had given
lack of clerical assistance in taking care of
administrative and clerical duties as the reason
for little time devoted to curriculum development,
availability of such assistance, and even the
availability of help for curriculum development
was not significantly related to the principal's
attention to curriculum. Examining other reasons
given by principals for not devoting more time
to curriculum revealed that there was no relation
to the principal's autonomy in staff selection,
budget preparation, and instructional materials
selection.

    Finding that job conditions was not necessarily
the reason for little attention to curriculum

development by principals, he then turned to graduate preparation of individuals. Here he found two strong associations. Of those "most committed" to curriculum development, all had at least six credit-hours of coursework in curriculum development. Of those "least committed" only 40 percent reported having at least six credit-hours in curriculum. When asked how well their graduate coursework had prepared them for curriculum development again all of those "most committed" reported theirs was adequate, while only 67 percent of those "least committed" said theirs was adequate.

The one variable tested in the study found to be significant by Vann was that of the perception the principal had of what was considered important by central office superiors. Principals allocated their time to curriculum development according to the importance placed on this by their superiors. Vann thus concluded that principals give little time to curriculum development because they perceive this to be a relatively low priority of their superiors.

Vann sees two areas of improvement. Graduate schools of education should give more attention to curriculum development in the training of principals, and more attention needs to be given to improved relations between principals and central office persons in regard to curriculum development.

THE MEASUREMENT OF ADMINISTRATIVE COMPETENCIES

Walters, Donald L. Phi Delta Kappan, Volume 61, February 1980, pp. 423-425.

Walters presents the results of his analysis of four competency-based systems for assessing or measuring administrative competencies considered valuable to educational leaders. The systems are Educational Leadership Appraisal (ELA), The Georgia Principal Assessment System (GPAS),

Individual Learning Materials (ILM), and Special Education Supervisor Training (SEST) program.

The ELA consists of a set of situational exercises that may require a response by the individual acting alone or in a small group. The leadership dimensions included are management and organization, use of delegation, communication, problem solving, task orientation, and interpersonal qualities.

The GPAS consists of a set of instruments and procedures. The set of instruments, known as the Principal Performance Description Survey, includes four parts: 1) the Principal Form, with which the principal records self-perception of how often and how well 100 job related tasks are performed; 2) the Teacher Form, eliciting teacher perceptions of how often and how well the principal performs 64 job-related tasks with which teachers should be familiar; 3) the External Observer Form, a structured interview of the principal providing a rating of the degree to which "observable evidence" corroborates the principal's responses; and 4) the Superintendent Form eliciting the superintendent's perception of how well the principal performs on 42 dimensions of behavior.

The ILM is designed for individual competency-based education. Beginning with a self assessment test in either a course of graduate study or inservice program, the individual selects which modules to study and the level of competency to be acquired. Available modules encompass the areas of improvement of teaching, instructional supervision, planning and administration of educational programs, and the principalship.

The SEST program is based upon the assumption that certain competencies are required of all educational leaders. It uses a battery of five instruments: 1) Critical Competency Performance Inventory, utilizing statements describing 24 critical competencies sorted into categories reflecting the individual's performance levels;

2) Major Competency Assessment Inventory, assessing performance on 81 competencies which are components or subdivisions of the critical competencies; 3) Competency-Keyed Experience Inventory, containing a check-list of 158 activities related to the 24 critical competencies; 4) Knowledge Assessment Test, a multiple choice test of cognition keyed to the critical competencies; and 5) the Critical Competency Interest Scale, requiring the individual to rank-order the 24 critical competencies according to the relative importance of each to his professional growth.

Walters summarizes his investigation by stating that all four systems were designed to be used with inservice administrators; that only two (ILM and SEST) had been used in preservice training programs, but in neither case has a major portion of the training program been competency based, and that only one system (GPAS) was designed specifically for use with school principals. He notes that the validity of the instruments was largely based on content validity judgment by experts and practitioners and that no measures of reliability were reported for any of the instruments. However, he surmises that the four systems described offer a rich resource from which new work may proceed.

OTHER REFERENCES

Awender, M. A. "The Principal's Leadership Role: Perceptions of Teachers, Principals, and Superintendents," Education, Volume 99, Winter 1978, pp. 172-179.

Beecher, Russell S. "Staff Evaluation: The Essential Administrative Task," Phi Delta Kappan, Volume 60, March 1979, pp. 515-517.

Brimm, Jack L., John Forgety, and Kenneth Sadler. "Principals' Attitudes. Student Absenteeism: A Survey Report," NASSP Bulletin, Volume 62, February 1978, pp. 65-69.

Byrnes, Charles R. "How a School Board Can Influence State Elections," Phi Delta Kappan, Volume 60, June 1979, p. 728.

Cooper, Bruce S., Gerald O. Dreyfuss, and Henry R. Boekhoff. "Incentives That Work: An Administrative Innovation in the Dade County Schools," Phi Delta Kappan, Volume 61, April 1980, pp. 523-524.

Freeman, Gary, Roberta C. Palmer, and Ann S. Ferren. "Team Building for Supervisory Support," Educational Leadership, Volume 37, January 1980, pp. 356-357.

Goldman, Paul and Sundra Gregory. "Instituting PPBS in Schools: A Comparison of Two Districts," Urban Education, Volume 14, April 1979, pp. 76-90.

Gray, Frank and Margaret L. Burns. "Does 'Management by Objectives' Work in Education?" Educational Leadership, Volume 36, March 1979, pp. 414-417.

Herman, Jerry J. "How and Why a School District Implemented MBO," NASSP Bulletin, Volume 62, May 1978, pp. 82-88.

Jenkins, John M. "The Teacher-Adviser: An Old Solution Looking for a Problem," NASSP Bulletin, Volume 61, September 1977, pp. 29-34.

Jordon, Lucille G. "Systematizing Curricular Planning and Implementation: What a Supervisor Can Do," Educational Leadership, Volume 36, October 1978, pp. 41-45.

Kostman, Samuel. "On-the-Job Training for Classroom Supervisors," NASSP Bulletin, Volume 62, December 1978, pp. 44-50.

Mazzoni, Tim L. and Van D. Mueller. "School District Planning for Enrollment Decline: The Minnesota Approach," Phi Delta Kappan, Volume 61, February 1980, pp. 406-410.

Morgan, Stanley R. "Shared Governance: A Concept for Public Schools," NASSP Bulletin, Volume 64, January 1980, pp. 29-33.

Solo, Leonard, "Sharing the Power in a Public School," National Elementary Principal, Volume 58, March 1979, pp. 71-75.

Summers, Alex. "Angels in Purgatory: Los Angeles Awaits Two Decisions on Mandatory Busing for Desegregation," Phi Delta Kappan, Volume 60, June 1979, pp. 718-723.

Taylor, Raymond G., Jr. "If I Were Boss ..." Education, Volume 99, Fall 1978, pp. 8-9.

Weaver, Frances and Jeffry Gordon. "Staff Development Needs of Department Heads," Educational Leadership, Volume 36, May 1979, pp. 578-580.

Weingast, David. "Shared Leadership - 'The Damn Thing Works,'" Educational Leadership, Volume 37, March 1980, pp. 502-506.

CHAPTER III

TEACHERS: INSTRUCTIONAL ASPECTS

Observers of the educational scene of the past two decades have witnessed many innovative approaches to modify and improve both preservice and inservice education for classroom teachers. Various programs have been established to update and strengthen the teaching profession. Pushed by declining enrollments in certain areas of the country and tighter budgets, both institutions of higher education and local school districts have placed increasing importance on both pre-service and inservice education programs. From the time of the establishment of the first public normal school in America in 1839, preservice education programs have undergone many modifications, but a common thread has run through the program over the years. That thread is the close working relationship between the teacher education program and the local school district, the partnership which has survived many theoretical and practical modifications.

Advocates of current teacher education programs stress the importance of quality over quantity through competency-based teacher education programs/performance-based teacher certification, teacher centers, staff development strategies, and improved teacher evaluation techniques. There is a continuing interest in microteaching, evaluation by videotape, and the application of computer technology in certain programs. Many educators believe that good teachers develop their competence during the course of experience. Even if their preservice program was superior, teachers still need a strong inservice program to maintain their competencies. Some regional accreditation associations now require that all professional personnel earn additional units of instructional credit periodically either through inservice units or graduate programs in institutions of higher education. As a guide, strong inservice programs

can be designed to make teachers masters of the
subjects they teach, familiar with new classroom
materials and approaches, or better informed on
working with handicapped students.

Competency-based/performance-based teacher
education programs have been designed to strengthen
preservice teachers, beginning teachers, and
experienced teachers. Many programs around the
country stress field experiences, developmental
progress, continuous input from those working in
the program, more systematic evaluation, and a
community philosophy of education. Field centered
programs provide closer working relationships
between teacher education institutions and the
local school district. Although these competency/
performance based programs have gained acceptance,
other teacher educators prefer a more traditional
program or a combination competency-based/
traditional program utilizing the strengths from
each. Many colleges and universities have established teaching centers whether the emphasis is
on a competencies approach or traditional approach.
The teaching center is designed for many levels of
experiences for both preservice and inservice
teachers usually with a full time university
faculty member who teaches and coordinates the
program. This type teaching center is a classic
example of university-public school cooperation.

Another inservice innovation is the federal
Teacher Center Law which has recently become fully
operational. Teachers across the country can
submit proposals for the formation of a teacher
center. At a teacher center, the teachers can
form a Teacher Center Policy Board and develop a
program based on a teacher needs assessment study.
Many educators would like to see each Congressional
district have at least one teacher center to serve
teachers of that area. The programs of the teacher
center can be designed to offer the most practical
and helpful knowledge and skills to local teachers.
Teacher exchange programs are also promoted by
federal projects and local school systems as a
means of providing practical in-service education.

Staff development strategies are being
incorporated into preservice and inservice
programs through improved supervisory methods
and internship programs. Some institutions have
developed year long internships where the interns
are paid by the local school district. These
programs have strengthened both prospective
teachers and the experienced teachers working
with them. Staff development, as utilized in
these programs and others that stress supervisory
skills, is a positive approach to bringing about
necessary and fundamental changes when confidence
in educators and schools has eroded over the
years. Most staff development programs are a
professional response to the demands of the public
for more accountability in education. Examples
of successful inservice programs are the National
Writing Project, the National Diffusion Network,
and the Advanced Placement Program where workshops,
consultation, and materials have reached a high
level of staff productivity.

Improved teacher evaluation techniques are
closely related to competency-based education and
performance-based certification. Numerous research
efforts and study groups have designed evaluation
materials to produce a more systematic approach to
preservice and inservice teachers. Taking the best
from the elements of trait, behavioral, and
situational theories of teaching, researchers
across the country are working on better ways to
assess teachers and the teaching act. From interaction analysis to performance instruments, the
search for better teacher evaluation continues.

Teacher education observers have also noted
the utilization of computer technology, microteaching, and videotaping as methods of strengthening both young and experienced teachers. Although
used primarily with undergraduate teacher education
programs, some districts and universities are now
employing these techniques to assist in improving
the classroom instruction of experienced teachers.
These programs usually rely on a systems analysis

approach and provide individual assistance to the teachers involved.

Teacher education programs at both the pre-service and inservice levels should provide, as a minimum, a greater depth of knowledge of subject area content and training in development of specialized skills. Both preservice and inservice education stand in need of improved programs. Professionals in education need skills in learning to define the objectives of teacher education programs, to articulate a professional sequence of laboratory experiences both in the classroom and field, to evaluate and counsel preservice and inservice teachers, and to share responsibility between the colleges of education and local schools in the process of teacher education. The various challenges and pressures of accountability, federal aid, technology, professionalism, and staff development have forced teachers to examine all facets of instruction. The development and maintenance of more competent, professional teach-ers is one of the major goals of thoughtful educators. The teaching profession has learned many lessons as it coped with the problems of the 1960's and 1970's. A revitalized professional experience sequence can strengthen the teaching profession even under adverse conditions by maintaining instructional improvement as a top priority in the immediate future.

SYNOPSES

APPLICATION OF COMPUTER TECHNOLOGY IN UNDER-
GRADUATE TEACHER EDUCATION

Askov, Eunice N., Jane Single, and Michael Clemens.
English Education, Volume 9, Winter 1978,
pp. 102-109.

The authors report that the College of
Education of Pennsylvania State University has
developed a program of Competency Based Teacher
Education (CBTE) that relies heavily on computer
assistance for effective instruction. In two
courses, Language Education 400 and 441, the
development and assessment of knowledge level
behavioral objectives and the clerical work of
tracking student progress through all objectives
is handled by computer. In some areas simulation
level behavioral objectives are also taught by
computer.

Three program systems are employed in the
Penn State program. The Computer Assisted
Instruction System teaches and tests knowledge
level objectives. The Computer Managed Instruction System records and processes mass student
data relative to the CBTE programs. The Instruction
Support System coordinates the other two systems
and performs a variety of computation tasks needed
for diagnostic-prescriptive and evaluative variants
as well as individualized record-keeping and varied
feedback control.

The program benefits students, faculty, and
administrators alike. Students keep track of their
progress on a daily and weekly basis. Faculty
members are able to give more attention to simulation level and field level evaluations because
most knowledge level assessments are handled by
computer. Administrators can more easily keep
track of instruction effectiveness. Because of
the time demands of a full CBTE program on both
students and faculty, computer assistance is
almost required, especially with large numbers of
students.

52

Computer assistance has enabled teachers to teach and personally evaluate student progress without being continually involved in the clerical tasks of education. Quick feedback has enabled teachers and students to succeed more fully and positively in this Competency Based Teacher Education Program at Pennsylvania State University.

BEYOND STUDENT TEACHING

Brimm, Jack L. and James K. Dotson. _Tennessee Teacher_, Volume 46, March 1979, pp. 17-19.

Brimm and Dotson describe a year long Teaching Internship Program (TIP) developed and implemented at Tennessee Technological University six years ago as an alternative to the existing one quarter long student teaching experience. In this program interns are involved in a three quarter certification experience at a contracted salary of $380-$450 monthly. Six quarter hours are earned each quarter. While the majority of students still elect the traditional program, more than 100 interns have been placed in schools in Tennessee and surrounding states.

Interns become a part of the regular school staff and begin the school year with inservice sessions. As faculty members, interns attend all staff meetings and extracurricular functions and in the classroom, the intern is viewed as a teaching associate while gradually developing into a teacher with full time duties. One eastern Tennessee school system uses the team concept with a team consisting of four members, three certified teachers and one intern.

The program has had some financial problems since each local system usually funds the interns and funds are tight at times. Also, for the university the program is relatively high-cost because of travel expenses and staff time. Despite these financial problems, the staff at Tennessee Tech is convinced that the year long

53

internship program provides many benefits for the university, the school system, and the intern. The interns, in essence, are members of the local school system staff rather than the traditional part time student teacher.

BREAKING AWAY FROM THE TRADITIONAL METHODS CLASS

Dean, Roger and Marian Demand. Music Educators Journal, Volume 63, May 1977, pp. 44-47.

Dean and Demand report on a university extern program for sophomore music education majors at Temple University in Pennsylvania. Temple University has developed an extern program for sophomore music education majors enrolled in "Music in the Elementary School." In addition to the regular class sessions, each extern, beginning in the fifth week, is actively involved in the instruction of elementary students once a week.

In the program the purpose of music in the public schools is defined as a part of aesthetic education. The student becomes aware that producing, analyzing, conceptualizing, and evaluating music are processes in which perception and reaction can take place. The next step is to develop a framework allowing the student to establish goals and order the sequence of events within a lesson while developing a comprehensive lesson plan. Externs are encouraged to evaluate their lessons in light of music competencies they have formulated and in terms of other significant developments occurring within the lesson.

Teaching assignments are carried out in two inner-city schools close to campus, one public and the other parochial. Neither of the two schools has a certified general music teacher. After several small group experiences, an extern is ready to encounter a large group of children. Experience has indicated that working with a small group helps to prepare the extern for a large group assignment.

Evaluation of extern teaching is accomplished in several ways. The most effective is the conference that the college instructor has with the extern immediately following the lesson. Notes taken by an observing classroom teacher also furnish material for discussion of those techniques that produced good results and those that did not. Externs are also video-taped during the semester and a private viewing arranged for purpose of self-evaluation. This extern program enables the student to become engaged in the teaching process early and assists in determining the professional attitudes and commitment to teaching.

A FACULTY-INITIATED INSERVICE PROGRAM

Dieter, Lynn and John Crouser. NASSP Bulletin, Volume 61, January 1977, pp. 111-112.

Dieter and Crouser report on an inservice program initiated by a high school faculty. Recognizing the need for better communication between departments and among the faculty themselves, the faculty of Main Township High School East in Park Ridge, Illinois developed a successful inservice program that helped alleviate communication problems. The program, which was initiated by concerned faculty members, was planned by a committee consisting of teachers, the principal, and two members of the Illinois Human Relations Commission. To initiate the organizational meetings, the principal sent personal notes to teachers rather than the usual memos. During the planning sessions teachers expressed complaints about too much departmentalization, teacher problems, and administrative ambiguity.

The first inservice workshop, which met with mixed reaction, consisted of two communication exercises: acquainting faculty members with each other and assisting them in working on group consensus tasks. The exercises involved groups

of ten to twelve teachers representing various
departments. To plan the second workshop, the
organizational committee recruited new faculty
members. The emphasis of the second workshop
was on issues important to the total school
program; and to deal with these issues, each
group of teachers designed a four-year program
for a hypothetical student. After they had
designed their programs, the group members
discussed how consensus was reached and how
the group members worked. Before the third
inservice workshop, faculty members filled out
information sheets listing their hobbies, skills,
and areas of expertise. As a result, the third
workshop utilized school personnel to conduct
mini-courses in areas as diverse as school law
to audiovisual aids. The third workshop was
completely successful and enthusiastically
received.

Dieter and Crouser suggest that their inservice program is a good model for others to
follow, especially since it puts into practice
the educational theory that the continuing
education of a faculty should begin with the
faculty. The positive responses from the workshop
method indicate that this approach has good
inservice potential.

SOLVING A COMMON PROBLEM: GRADUATE EDUCATION
   FOR TEACHERS

Douglas, Lawrence H.   Kappa Delta Pi Record,
   Volume 14, April 1978, pp. 114-115.

Douglas reports that many teacher training
institutions now lack students from their
immediate location for their graduate programs
and he discusses a "two-summer" approach designed
to attract students to graduate study. The
Department of Education at Plymouth State College,
New Hampshire, attempts to solve its problem of
how a small graduate program operating many miles
from any sizeable population base might attract

new students to its program by making the required
courses and electives available to students for
the Master's of Education degree over a fourteen
month period including two summers and an interim
year.

The major concerns addressed in developing
the program were time, cost, and curriculum.
Time for the program was set at fourteen months,
rather than the usual four or five years. Cost
was held to a minimum and course offerings were
realigned to accommodate the new program. Students
interested in the two-summer program apply for
admission prior to the summer they wish to start
the program. They complete 12 semester hours
during Sessions II and III of the first summer.
While they are teaching during the interim year,
they enroll in either a practicum in administration
and supervision or an independent study course
with the Plymouth State Faculty. During this year
they also earn six additional credits. Then the
students return the second summer to finish their
course work and complete program requirements.

The program has been well received by teachers
throughout New Hampshire and in adjoining states.
The results of this experimentation have been
positive and the college is now in its third
cycle of the program. The Two-Summer Master's
Program has offered the college a new way of
looking at its students and has provided valuable
insight into its program management.

THE SYRACUSE UNIVERSITY TEACHER CENTER: A MODEL
    FOR PRESERVICE/INSERVICE

Evans, Robert L. and Alvah Kilgore. Phi Delta
    Kappan, Volume 59, April 1978, pp. 538-541.

Evans and Kilgore describe a preservice/
inservice development program instituted at
Syracuse University which has involved the city
school district, the local community, the teachers
association, and the university. The approach

includes development of three teaching centers whose primary aim is to integrate preservice and inservice education. The program originated from two sources. The New York State Board of Regents mandated that each school of education develop a competency-based teacher education program. Along with this, the National Teacher Corps program set up guidelines which state that the project must involve cooperation between the local community, the institution of higher learning, and the local education agency. The governing structure of the Syracuse Urban Teaching Center (SUTC) is made up of university faculty and administrators, school district faculty and administrators, and community members.

The Center holds classes, workshops, and seminars which focus on issues of importance to community residents. One course involved a parent effectiveness program. One workshop was presented for community members, teachers, and administrators to determine how best to relate to the three major environments in which a child lives - the school, the home, and the community.

The SUTC is centrally located between five center schools and serves as a meeting place for inservice programs, workshops, and a resource base for materials, books, and supplies. Student teachers are an integral part of the teaching center which is staffed by volunteer teachers.

The heart of the teaching center is the development of preservice and inservice programs. Preservice students receive the field-based portion of their training within the center schools under the supervision of a center coordinator. The inservice linkage between Syracuse University and the center schools revolves around the participation of Syracuse University faculty who offer academic courses for teachers and parents in the center schools. They also work individually with center teachers in the classroom.

58

It is expected that these preservice/inservice programs will provide teachers with new and additional skills which would have a positive effect on student learning. The SUTC is an example of a teaching center making a difference in an urban setting.

FROM TRADITIONAL TO COMPETENCY-BASED TEACHER
    EDUCATION AND BACK AGAIN: AN EIGHT-YEAR
    EXPERIMENT

Lorber, Michael A.   Phi Delta Kappan, Volume 60,
    March 1979, pp. 523-524.

Lorber describes the students and resources that went into an eight-year Illinois State University (ISU) program, its results and implications. The ISU program, entitled the Professional Sequence, involved thousands of prospective secondary school teachers who were involved in a program which was converted from a traditional format to a comprehensive self-paced competency-based format. Students enrolled in the Professional Sequence were typical education majors who were drawn from the top half of their high school graduating classes and had completed two years of university level work. They were pursuing state certification in the secondary grades through the program.

Resources available to faculty and students in this program included the full resources of the university, library media production specialists, reading and writing clinics, and health/counseling services. The program was staffed by approximately seven professors and two graduate assistants. The program also used the departmental clerical staff, the testing center, a computerized record-keeping system, a simulated teaching laboratory with 12 stations equipped with video-tape recorders, and an excellent random-access information retrieval system.

The Professional Sequence faculty attempted

to build a program characterized by objectives related to planning, teaching, and evaluating with sufficient flexibility and time to accommodate the varying learning rates and styles of students.

An analysis of both formal and informal program evaluations led to the conclusion that the single-format, self-paced competency-based program did not adequately meet the varying instructional needs of the students. About 25% of the students were unable or unwilling to pace their own learning effectively; another 25%, primarily the older and/or married students, used self-pacing effectively. The bulk of the students displayed varying self-pacing abilities but generally tended to seek more structured alternatives when such alternatives were made available. Thus, a move back to the traditional format was made.

Illinois State University undertook its self-paced, competency-based program under what appeared to be nearly ideal conditions with respect to students, faculty, resources, and program design. Nonetheless, major programmatic changes were needed. The four most pervasive and difficult problems that had to be solved in the ISU program were 1) how to meet the varying instructional needs of large numbers of students, 2) how to provide uniform evaluation of any but the cognitive skills at the lowest level, 3) how to encourage excellence with a pass-fail reward system, and 4) how to permit academic freedom with respect to teaching and research while maintaining a specific set of program goals, content, and procedures.

COLLEGES AND UNIVERSITIES WORKING ON TEACHER
    EDUCATION STANDARDS

Ohio Schools, Volume 58, February 1978, pp. 19-21.

The editors report that the Ohio State Board

of Education adopted new standards, December 1974, effective in all Ohio teacher training institutions in 1980. In order to monitor how the various colleges and universities are complying with the new standards, the Ohio State Department of Education has been conducting a series of visitations at all teacher training institutions. In 1978, each institution reported to the State Department its progress in meeting the new standards and visitation teams were assigned to verify these reports.

The visitation teams consisted of classroom teachers who were trained for the assessment job in workshops conducted by the Ohio Education Association's Teacher Education and Professional Standards (TEPS) Commission. By serving on the visitation teams, Ohio's teachers are able to insure that the new standards of particular interest to practicing teachers are being implemented and serve on advisory committees representing the schools which are the locations for field based experiences for individual institutions. Teachers develop the objectives and experiences for field-based experiences. They require that college teacher education personnel meet specific criteria before working with pre-service teachers.

The visitation teams have discovered that the biggest problems facing teacher training institutions are in developing their curricula. Consequently, the State Department of Education's Division of Teacher Education and Certification is encouraging them to develop a program of studies rather than to list some all-too-frequently unrelated courses. Clinical and field based experiences are being emphasized. The teacher evaluators also found that despite financial problems, the small colleges are progressing as well as the big colleges in bringing their standards into compliance.

61

TEACHER CENTERS - THE FRENCH MODEL

Oliva, Peter F. Florida Association of Supervision
    and Curriculum Development Journal, Volume 1,
    February 1979, pp. 21-25.

    Oliva reports on and compares French teacher
centers with American teacher centers. The
author describes three Regional Centers for
Pedagogical Documentation (CRDP) in Orleans,
Toulouse, and Grenoble. In all three he discovered
a variety of programs and services that could
provide suggestions for American teacher education
centers. Oliva makes the point that teacher
education centers developing in the United States
are more a concept than a structure with no
buildings of their own and a small staff. The main
emphasis is usually on in-service education.

    The French centers differ in that they are
more teacher service centers than teacher education
centers. The French centers might be conceptual-
ized as a combination professional library, media
center, conference center, consulting agency,
teacher training center, educational press,
curriculum laboratory, research agency, and book-
store with emphasis on service to teachers of the
area. The CRDP's in France serve primarily the
secondary schools of the area through the library/
media specialists who run each school's Center
for Documentation and Information. Elementary
schools receive little service, although the
center staff goes to normal schools periodically
to conduct workshops.

    Oliva proposes teacher education centers in
the United States modeled after the French centers
by providing a wider range of services. These
centers would respond to needs of the teachers
of a certain area and would at the same time try
to stimulate both curricular and instructional
improvements. He suggests that a few teachers
on special assignment could be assigned to a center
for a year at a time. One of the biggest hurdles
to clear would be the provision of quarters for

the center. The author concludes that the ultimate goal of a teacher center is improvement in the curriculum and instruction with resulting improvement in student achievement. Combining the strengths of the French teacher center with the American model is worthy of exploration at this time.

IN SEARCH OF MR. (MS.) GOODTEACHER

Reynolds, John C. Action in Teacher Education, Volume 2, Winter 1979-80, pp. 35-38.

Reynolds reports on the background of teacher effectiveness and a current program at the University of Georgia which combines the most effective elements of many teacher effectiveness studies. The author discussed research studies of the 1940's, 1950's, and 1960's which could be classified as trait, behavioral, and situational theories. Taking certain elements of these theories, a University of Georgia research team, directed by Charles Johnson, has developed the Teacher Performance Assessment Instruments (TPAI) for utilization by student teachers and beginning teachers in the state of Georgia as mandated by the state legislature.

The advances made in teacher effectiveness research studies have led to a performance-based criteria concept over the past few years. As a specific example, the TPAI incorporates 16 generic competencies which are assessed through a number of highly specific indicators and descriptors designed by the University of Georgia research team.

Reynolds recognizes the complexities involved in evaluating teacher effectiveness, but this article provides a rationale and a specific example of a practical approach to identifying effective classroom teachers in the 1980's. The four factors emerging from past and present research studies which generally differentiate

effective teachers from ineffective teachers are
superior personality organization, good judgment/
reasoning, capacity to relate to others, and a
knowledge of basic content and instructional
methods. Although the search for effective
teachers continues, the author points out that
teacher effectiveness is inherently difficult
to assess because of the long range outcomes
built into the basic act of teaching.

THE EAST RAMAPO TEACHERS' CENTER

Rosenblatt, Linda. Today's Education, Volume 68,
    April-May 1979, pp. 36-37.

Rosenblatt reports on the East Ramapo
Teachers' Center which was one of three such
centers funded in New York State. This center
was set up and truly managed by teachers with
all its programs designed by participating teachers. The center is open until five o'clock on
school days, longer if a class or a meeting is
scheduled,and on Saturdays.

The Center set forth six major goals from
the beginning. They are 1) facilitating the
transfer of handicapped students into a regular
school program through a program of strategies
designed and delivered by teachers; 2) improving
the instructional program of students who speak
English as a second language; 3) developing a
set of strategies for putting the district's
new mathematics curriculum into practice;
4) developing a sequential writing program for
grades 7 through 12; 5) encouraging teachers to
participate in the center's activities through
a systematic, ongoing communications and public
relations program; and 6) providing continuous
opportunities for teachers to meet, solve problems,
exchange ideas, and develop their own materials
for classroom use.

According to Rosenblatt, the center moved
progressively toward meeting these goals. Teachers

planned and presented the math strategies course.
Another teacher organized a course on teaching
handicapped students. The Center offered mini-
courses from learning games to values clarification. Teachers come to attend scheduled workshops,
to make classroom materials, to read, or get
ideas. Karen Wilson, Center Director, estimates
that between 300 and 400 teachers have become
involved so far. In assessing the East Ramapo
Center after one year, the findings were positive
in all respects between the Center and the
community.

TAKING INSERVICE EDUCATION OFF THE BACK BURNER

Seldin, Clement A. Phi Delta Kappan, Volume 61,
     December 1979, pp. 266,287.

     Seldin reports on an effort in Western
Massachusetts to develop useful staff development
programs for public school personnel. The School
of Education at the University of Massachusetts,
the Springfield Regional Education Center, and
the Hampshire Educational Collaborative were all
interested in a means to determine inservice
needs. The three agencies worked together to
design and conduct a major needs survey of area
educators. A two-page questionnaire was piloted
to insure quality; contacts were made with seven
district superintendents. Out of 880 questionnaires distributed to school personnel, 615
were completed and returned. The questionnaire
solicited preferences for the following: format,
location, time, length, instructor, subject
matter, and credit for inservice education.

     After needs of the public school personnel
had been identified, the three sponsoring agencies
collaborated on ways to address those needs.
They decided to address one of the important
issues, programs for gifted and talented. The
three agencies then planned a conference on this
topic. The response to this conference was both
positive and overwhelming. This gratifying

65

response would seem to mandate further action.
Thus, the major needs survey has become important
in providing inservice needs in Western Massachusetts.

ANALYZING EDUCATIONAL PLATFORMS: A SUPERVISORY
    STRATEGY

Simon, Alan E. Educational Leadership, Volume 34,
    May 1977, pp. 580-584.

    Simon reports on a four-stage process using
videotaping as a feed-back tool based on the
assumption that a teacher's classroom behavior
can differ from that same teacher's beliefs about
education. A group of professors at the University
of Illinois have developed a four-stage process of
giving useful feedback to teachers using videotaping. The first stage focuses in on how the
teacher wants to relate to the instructional
task through an interview about the teaching
situation that follows. The second stage seeks
to clarify the first stage as a supervisor or
another teacher asks questions. These questions
focus on the teacher's plan of action as seen by
another person. The third stage involves viewing the videotaped lesson. A teacher and a
supervisor work together to reconstruct what
actually happened. The final stage is designed
to scrutinize and search out with questions how
the teaching process can be brought closer to
what the teacher intended it to be.

    The author states that after teachers learn
the techniques of self improvement using videotaped feedback this tool can then be used
independently. Other applications of the same
technique are suggested. Superintendents and
principals could use the technique to analyze
meetings. Graduate students could practice with
other students, professors, or student teachers.

    Enthusiasts are warned by Simon not to
depend on videotaping as the only means of

supervision or self-improvement. The camera sees only part of the interaction taking place. This is not a complete documentation of a classroom interaction. However, videotaping a teacher's interaction with students is providing valuable feedback to teachers in this situation. An organized four-stage approach has been used successfully. This approach emphasizes the theory of what is to take place and then analyzes teacher practice, relating it back to theory.

FROM TRADITIONAL TO COMPETENCY-BASED TEACHER EDUCATION--AND NEVER BACK AGAIN

Smith, Hayden R. and Thomas S. Nagel. Phi Delta Kappan, Volume 61, November 1979, pp. 194-195.

Smith and Nagel describe a successful Competency-Based Teacher Education (CBTE) program at San Diego State University. The article is written as a rebuttal to Lorber's report that CBTE had failed at Illinois State University. The attitude at San Diego State has been one of placing student welfare before faculty comfort and the authors report that this is a key factor in a successful program that has been in effect for eight years.

Although recognizing that CBTE remains controversial, Smith and Nagel note that opposition to CBTE arises from two major sources: it requires a great deal more work on the part of the faculty and it forces a drastic instructional change on the faculty. The San Diego State University CBTE program's success has been attributed to its variety. No single department is completely competency-based, but all seven departments from elementary and secondary to educational technology/librarianship and the community college program have either bachelor's or master's degree programs based on the CBTE approach. The move to a competency-based format was not mandated; it was purely voluntary. The cooperative quality of the program has been a strength.

In summary, Smith and Nagel state that anyone who has used a CBTE approach effectively can never return to a traditional way of teaching. They base this on the assumption that CBTE provides for total involvement which is the touchstone of teaching effectiveness and the individual instructor at San Diego State or elsewhere reaches a point of no turning back as the individual becomes more involved in CBTE.

STRENGTHENING THE TEACHING PROFESSION THROUGH SUPERVISING TEACHING ASSESSMENT

Reynolds, John C., Lutian R. Wootton, and Charles S. Gifford. College Student Journal, Volume 12, Summer 1978, pp. 188-191.

Reynolds, Wootton, and Gifford report on the Competency-Based Supervising Teacher Program (CBSTP) currently in use at the University of Georgia. This program is an on-going example of the interface between behaviorism and humanism in preparing supervising teachers of student teachers. Beginning in 1974, the program has emphasized six major competencies and a self-evaluation technique utilized by the teachers and college supervisors in a humanistic approach to working with student teachers. This program was designed to strengthen the teacher education program through utilization of the strongest aspects of both behavioristic and humanistic theory.

The six major program areas for which competency statements were developed are 1) planning for working with a student teacher, 2) human relations skills, 3) professional and personal development, 4) philosophy of teaching and curriculum development, 5) school-community relationships, and 6) evaluation. These six major areas are further broken down into 22 competencies and 217 indicators for self-assessment.

Self-evaluation is a major emphasis in assessment of the college supervisor, the supervising teacher, and the student teacher in the University of Georgia. The CBSTP is a response to the environment created through a typical CBTE program. The emphasis is on a field-centered program which is functionally integrated into the teaching profession. Because of the practical features built into the program, the supervising teachers involved have provided positive responses to the CBSTP at the University of Georgia.

Other References

Barber, Carol. "Training Principals and Teachers for Mastery Learning," Educational Leadership, Volume 37, November 1979, pp. 126-127.

Chantland, Gloria Cosgrove. "Teaching Is Loving Something So Much," Today's Education, Volume 68, September-October 1979, pp. 73, 86.

Cortis, Gerald and Anne Grayson. "Primary School Pupils' Perceptions of Student Teachers' Performance," Educational Review, Volume 30, February 1978, pp. 93-101.

Estes, Swain M. "Professional Development Center," Texas Outlook, Volume 62, March 1978, pp. 58-59.

Goddu, Roland, Jeannie Crosby, and Sara Massey. "Inservice: The Professional Development of Educators," Journal of Teacher Education, Volume 28, March-April, 1977, pp. 24-30.

Gonder, Peggy Odell. "Training Teachers to Teach Writing," American Education, Volume 15, April 1979, pp. 33-38.

Gubser, Lyn. "Competency Testing and National Accreditation in Teacher Education," Action in Teacher Education, Volume 1, Spring-Summer 1979, pp. 21-28.

Hargie, Owen. "The Effectiveness of Microteaching: A Selective Review," Educational Review, Volume 29, February 1977, pp. 87-95.

Kaser, Thomas. "American Exchange Teachers in Britain - Good Show!," Today's Education, Volume 67, September-October 1978, pp. 50-52.

Kimmel, Ellen, Dorothy Harlow, and Mary Topping. "Training Women for Administrative Roles," Educational Leadership, Volume 37, December 1979, pp. 229-231.

McComb, Don and Alan Willsey. "So You're Interested in Teaching Centers," Today's Education, Volume 67, April-May 1978, p. 69.

Perrone, Vito. "Supporting Teacher Growth," Childhood Education, Volume 54, April-May 1978, pp. 298-302.

Pietras, Thomas P. "Modification of Preservice Teacher Attitudes Through Analysis of Films," Peabody Journal of Education, Volume 55, January 1978, pp. 127-130.

Reilly, Wayne. "Competency-Based Education: Pros and Cons," American Education, Volume 14, April 1978, pp. 21-23, 26.

Robinson, Paul. "Preprofessional Laboratories: Know-How for Future Teachers," Kappa Delta Pi Record, Volume 14, April 1978, pp. 107-108.

Weaver, W. Timothy. "In Search of Quality: The Need for Talent in Teaching," Phi Delta Kappan, Volume 61, September 1979, pp. 29-32.

Zirkel, Perry A. and Victoria F. Albert. "Assessing Teachers' Preferences Regarding Inservice Education," Clearing House, Volume 52, March 1979, pp. 328-333.

CHAPTER IV
TEACHERS: NON-INSTRUCTIONAL ASPECTS

The non-instructional aspects of teaching have a profound effect on teachers. Beginning teachers usually learn quite early in their teaching careers about these non-instructional aspects. In the past two decades, non-instructional aspects of teaching have played an increasingly important role for classroom teachers. There are two broad categories affecting teachers. The first is the battered teacher syndrome including teacher stress/burnout, violence directed against teachers, hazards associated with teaching, and the maintenance of positive mental health in extremely trying circumstances. The second category is the legalistic syndrome affecting teachers which includes state mandates on curriculum programs, legal decision, tenure, certification/recertification laws, controversy surrounding textbooks, censorship, grievance arbitrations, school closings, and teacher rights.

Since World War II, schools and teachers have been called upon to provide assistance for the ills of contemporary society. State and federal legislation has mandated that teachers become involved in child nutrition, working with the handicapped, in promoting racial equality, developing bilingual and bicultural programs, dropout prevention, and community projects. The school lunch program is a classic example of schools taking over a family function as ordered by federal law. In common with federal programs, this program calls for increased paperwork, changing guidelines, and regulatory practices. Thus, teachers become involved in many programs and school functions which are not instructional by nature.

Teacher stress/burnout is a major problem in today's classroom and it seems to be growing. This occurs when stress, tension, and anxiety override the positive feelings about teaching. The incidence of violence and vandalism is increasing. According to an NEA survey, an estimated 110,000 teachers were physically assaulted on school property during the 1978-79 academic year. In addition to this violence, teacher burnout is also caused by disruptive students, salary problems, school closings, excessive paperwork, large classes, and lack of parental support. As a result, teachers are leaving the profession in great numbers to pursue other types of employment. The nature of the teaching profession contributes to certain mental health pressures because of the trying circumstances of many teaching situations across the country exemplified by the large class - several classes per day required of high school programs and in elementary programs where teachers have no relief from children all day. Educators now face the difficult task of preventing or easing teacher burnout through counseling programs and other appropriate means. Teachers can work together to establish better mental health by sharing ideas, methods, and materials which may make teaching easier and more enjoyable. Support and cooperation from fellow teachers and administrators also helps reduce some of the stress from the teaching profession.

The legal aspects surrounding teachers today comprise the second broad category, the legalistic syndrome. Teachers are vitally affected by court decisions, legislative mandates, certification laws, censorship, controversial issues, and grievance arbitrations/strikes. Teacher strikes are a continuing phenomena characterized by closed schools, unrest among teachers, and parental anger. The overriding strike issues are usually money and class size. Most teachers report that they have yet to see reported declining enrollments translated into reduced class size and better opportunities for teaching. School closings and loss of educational funding from legislative acts also affect teachers in many ways. These problems have led to increased emphasis on contract negotiations in recent years. These negotiations have included discipline improvements, job security, more time for planning, teacher evaluation methods, and dismissal problems.

State mandates on curriculum, controversial textbooks, and certain forms of censorship are also in the legalistic mold. These events usually are characterized by strong emotional feelings on the part of the general public. When concrete objects such as textbooks are tampered with, citizens respond more rapidly than they would on more abstract topics. Thus curriculum programs, textbook selection, and censorship of school materials become forces which the classroom teacher must deal with. To accomplish this in a straight forward, objective manner is not an easy task. Once again, classroom teachers need support and assistance in these controversial areas which are apparently on the increase across the country. When curriculum is mandated by state legislatures, teachers have to be familiar with the background and causes of the mandate no matter which subject content area or grade level is affected. This also applies to textbook selection and utilization. Censorship, in any form, requires that classroom teachers be knowledgeable about the materials involved, the background, the individuals involved, and the legal means available to take action.

Certification laws, recertification laws, and teacher evaluation techniques affect teachers in many ways. With an increase in more systematic accountability measures, new laws and techniques for certifying, recertifying, and evaluating teachers have become increasingly important to teachers. Teacher and administrator input is required in these areas along with external assistance as needed in individual cases.

The teachers of today require special skills in understanding the legal aspects of teaching whether these aspects related to the battered teacher or the teacher caught up in legal issues beyond the control of the individual. To master these skills, teachers have a need to be knowledgeable in the history of education, school law, current events, state/federal legislative actions, and judicial procedures at the lower and state levels. Powerful forces such as federal aid, increased accountability, more aware parents, involved state legislatures, and declining student enrollments have contributed and are continuing to contribute to the non-instructional aspects of teaching. Teachers must be knowledgeable in both instructional and non-instructional aspects during the coming years to cope with the legal, political, and economic factors involved with teaching.

In spite of the fact that community pressures on teachers are great, that salaries have not caught up much less kept pace with inflation, that teachers encounter physical violence, and that legal decisions and federal emphases have limited their ability to function fully as professional persons, there are some bright spots. Teachers are better organized than ever, and their collective efforts are netting increased financial support, educational improvement programs for personnel, better resources and facilities for teaching, and personal remuneration including salaries, health services, and retirement benefits.

SYNOPSES

THE PAIN OF TEACHER BURNOUT: A CASE HISTORY

Bardo, Pamela. Phi Delta Kappan, Volume 61,
    December, 1979, pp. 252-253.

Bardo describes her exit from the teaching
profession to become a stockbroker. She taught
at El Rancho High School in the Los Angeles area
long enough to be halfway to retirement with an
adequate salary and minimal classroom demands.
Why would she choose to leave? The author
explains that she was a victim of teacher burnout brought about by a feeling of despair and
hopelessness. Specifically, her American studies
team-teaching class which contained the school's
best and brightest students turned in no more than
half their assignments which were too hastily
prepared. In addition, the independent study
phase became a social gathering.

During her 17 years of teaching at a Southern
California high school, Bardo had learned to cope
with just about anything that came up. But, in
recent years, she began to notice that her
students were using the ultimate weapon against
the school, the teachers, and themselves: they
simply refused to do the work that leads to learning. Before leaving teaching, many teachers in
the school attempted to teach courses such as
"Mass Media" or "Books and Films" because of the
close relationship to movies and television. The
students responded by watching in these classes,
but not in analyzing, writing, or thinking. So
the teachers changed this tactic and revised
those classes in a "back to basics" push.

This is only one case history; however, a
recent NEA survey estimates that 30 percent of
American teachers would like to be doing something
else. The tremendous burden placed upon teachers
to be all things to all people is taking its toll
in the malady of teacher burnout.

TESTIMONY OF A BATTERED TEACHER

Campbell, Margaret H. Phi Delta Kappan, Volume
    60, February 1979, pp. 441-442.

Campbell describes an assault and the suffer-
ing associated with it since she was attacked
recently in a large urban high school. She was
hit over the head with a long, thick piece of
wood by a 15 year old female student who was
angered because the previous day the student
was removed from class for causing a serious
disturbance. The teacher was dazed and hurt
seriously enough to have to stay out of school
for five days. In addition to her physical
state, the teacher's mental state was not too
good, especially after the charge against the
student was changed from a felony to a misde-
meanor. Ultimately, the Board of Education
acted to expel "for life" the student who attacked
the author.

Campbell offers sound advice to any teacher who
is a victim of an assault and the actions the
school should take. Following are her suggestions:
1) call the police and prosecute the attacker;
2) provide medical help quickly and have an
administrator stay with the teacher during the
medical/legal procedures; 3) administrator should
provide support after medical attention has been
received; 4) each school should set up a support
team to help the assaulted teacher; 5) counseling
services should be provided; 6) the Board of
Education attorney should be available to help
in legal matters; 7) when the teacher returns to
work, much support should be provided; and
8) the Board of Education should follow-up and
find out if the assaulted teacher needs any
additional help.

SCHOOL CLOSINGS AFFECT TEACHERS - THE ALEXANDRIA,
    VIRGINIA, STORY

Cleveland, Marilyn J. and Tricia Gibbons. Today's

77

Education, Volume 69, February-March 1980,
pp. 45-47.

Cleveland and Gibbons report on the situation
in Alexandria, Virginia where six schools have
been closed since 1971 through integration,
declining enrollments, and consolidation. Many
factors are considered in consolidation including
declining birthrate, projected enrollment, local
tax rates, community attachments, and condition
of buildings. The authors maintain that the
factors needed to make the newly consolidated
schools work are the teachers and the instructional program. As professional educators,
teachers are concerned about curriculum changes,
class size, special programs, and children when
consolidation occurs.

School consolidation has two other important
effects on teachers' professional lives. There
are actual or threatened loss of teaching positions
and changes in assignment or teaching conditions.
In Alexandria, teachers received notices of their
new assignments in the consolidated schools or
they received "to be assigned" (TBA) notices which
upset many teachers. One teacher with 30 years
service was labeled TBA.

The authors point out that consolidation in
Alexandria or anywhere is not a numbers game,
but a persons game. Consolidation has forced
many teachers to reassess themselves, a type of
self-evaluation which has led many teachers to
clear goals and new enthusiasm. Others see the
change as a threat. How teachers cope with it
is closely related to how each, as an individual,
copes with change.

HOW STATE MANDATES AFFECT CURRICULUM

Committee on Youth Education for Citizenship.
    Educational Leadership, Volume 37, January
    1980, pp. 334-336.

The Committee on Youth Education for Citizenship conducted a study of curriculum mandates,
laws, and regulations as they are perceived in
five states - Texas, Illinois, Georgia, Pennsylvania, and California. The Committee was
interested in how teachers and administrators
found out about state curriculum mandates and
how much influence the mandates had on the
curriculum. After carefully studying laws,
they interviewed social studies teachers for
more indepth information. The findings suggest
that information on mandates in the five states
is conveyed through formal courses, administrators,
and general experience. The largest number of
teachers, 43 percent, learned from administrators
in their school district.

Both teachers and administrators say the
mandates have some effect, although the extent
varies from state to state in the area of law-
related education. In general, educators said
that they did not think social studies mandates
were a major factor in shaping the curriculum.
But about 66 percent felt the mandate had some
effect in helping, directing, reinforcing, and
requiring. Teachers in Texas and Georgia attached
the most importance to state mandates. All in
all, the findings showed that teachers and
administrators are rather comfortable with their
state mandates. They are not always fully aware
of them and do not think mandates have a very
strong influence, but they support the idea of
mandates. The Committee concludes by stating
that mandates will probably be a part of the
educational scene for some time to come.

TEACHER PARTICIPATION IN SCHOOL DECISION MAKING:
THE SAN JOSE TEACHER INVOLVEMENT PROJECT

Crockenberg, Vincent and Woodrow W. Clark, Jr.
    Phi Delta Kappan, Volume 61, October 1979,
    pp. 115-118.

Crockenberg and Clark report on a project
designed to train classroom teachers to participate

with their building principals in identifying and resolving local school problems and to sustain the involvement by implementing formal decision-making procedures at each school site. The California Teacher Involvement Project (TIP), initiated through the California Teachers Association and organized in cooperation with the San Jose Public Schools and the San Jose Teachers Association, was funded through the National Institute of Education (NIE) for three years.

The chief vehicle for operation was a faculty advisory council in each school which developed its own constitution, by laws, and/or standing rules for operation. Workshops served as a means of developing policies and training faculty for carrying out the project. Three recognized teacher leaders from each interested school were recruited to attend workshops on the development of school site decision-making mechanisms. These groups of teachers then trained the other teachers in their respective schools in the skills necessary to participate in building level decision-making. In all, about a dozen schools and approximately 120 teachers and administrators participated in TIP workshops throughout the funding period.

The authors report that workshops were utilized during the first year to assist the faculty in self-governance by establishing a faculty council and a school constitution. Workshops in the second and third years focused on the progress being made by individual schools, their special problems, and the details of writing formal constitutions for each school site.

Crockenberg and Clark report thirteen areas identified by TIP staff for teacher involvement in school decision-making of particular concern to teachers. Some of the areas included were school budget, inservice training, principal/ teacher relations, teacher personnel policies, curriculum content and philosophy, instructional materials and methods, and school procedures.

Levels of involvement on which the faculties could choose to operate were 1) recommendation, 2) information, 3) consultation, 4) approval, and 5) authorization. Accordingly, the faculty or staff council would act in an advisory capacity to the principal, be informed of the principal's decisions and in turn inform the rest of the faculty, be consulted about decisions and have the right to alter, approve, or reject them, and initiate decision making, with the principal offering ideas and suggestions. The principal was expected to administer the decisions of the council.

Crockenberg and Clark reported that the district superintendent support TIP from the beginning, and any conflict between principals and teachers as to instructional decision-making was resolved in most schools when the teachers and principals cooperated in drawing up school constitutions. They noted that by the middle of the second year building administrators had begun to participate seriously in the project, and TIP schools began to make great progress in developing and implementing their self governance mechanisms. By the end of the third year twelve schools had developed councils and constitutions providing for legitimate and effective faculty participation in a wide variety of decision-making areas.

TENURE: ANOTHER SACRED COW ABOUT TO BITE THE DUST

Freiwald, J. Leo. Phi Delta Kappan, Volume 61, September 1979, p. 50.

Freiwald describes a situation in which members of the United Teachers of Dade (UTD), Dade County, Florida, ratified a three year contract that would eliminate the possibility of tenure for all new teachers. This contract also affects those teachers in the first or second years of the three year probationary period required for a Florida continuing contract. The reasons for this move are both interesting and complex. With declining school populations and taxpayer revolts, tenure has become anathema to many citizens. In such a climate, the Florida state legislature includes tenure laws among a group of statutes which will cease to exist unless action is taken by the state legislature to extend or replace them.

To fill this void that would be left by the expiring statute, negotiators representing the Dade County schools and UTD came up with a "just cause/due process" package. The negotiators have been concerned with the inherent weakness of the Florida tenure law since teachers could be dismissed for a variety of reasons. The professional responsibility-accountability section of the Dade County Public Schools Contract includes a diagnostic-prescriptive approach to improving teaching performance within appropriate time frames. No part of this section may be used in a dismissal action and it further prohibits mass testing of teachers. The due process section deals with unacceptable teaching performance and provides for union representation and appeal. The Dade National Education Association affiliate, a rival of UTD, predicts potential abuses of the just cause/due process agreement.

Freiwald concludes by implying that changes in teacher tenure laws are on the way and not limited to Dade County, Florida. He notes that teachers in many places are now pinning greater hope for job protection on board-union contracts rather than on state tenure laws.

CONTROVERSIAL ENGLISH LESSONS AND THE LAW

Hoy, Alice Kathleen. English Journal, Volume 66, February 1977, pp. 21-24.

Hoy, in an attempt to examine the question relating to limitations imposed by recent court decisions on the language, methods, and materials of English teachers, reports on six recent court decisions in six different states. The author breaks down the various court decisions into categories determined by the criteria the courts used in deciding for or against the teacher in question. The five categories Hoy reports are the following: (1) whether the assignment or conduct has a serious educational purpose; (2) whether it is related to the maturity and background of the particular students; (3) whether there is any regulation prescribing such assignment or conduct; (4) whether any disturbance or disruption of the educational process resulted from such teacher action; and (5) whether the assignment or conduct adversely affected the person's functioning as a teacher.

As one specific example, an Alabama English teacher assigned Kurt Vonnegut's Welcome to the Monkey House to her junior English classes. The teacher was rebuked by her principal and superintendent for using materials condoning free sex and the systematic killing of older people. When the teacher stated that in good conscience she could not agree never to teach the story again, she was dismissed on the grounds that her presence was disruptive to the teaching situation. The Alabama court overturned the school board's decision and ordered the English teacher reinstated. The decision was based on the finding that there was nothing in Vonnegut's story that would render it obscene. The evidence also reflected that the assigning of the story was greeted with apathy by most of the students.

Hoy concludes that although the courts have never stated that academic freedom means the absence of all restraint, the courts have repeatedly demonstrated that teachers who adhere to specified limits are protected by law.

83

TEACHER VERSUS ADMINISTRATOR

Hoyle, John R. Planning and Changing, Volume 9,
    Winter 1978, pp. 203-209.

Hoyle describes a one day workshop he
conducted which was sponsored by the Department
of Educational Administration at the University
of Akron. The group of 250 administrators and
supervisors were there to explore the growing
crisis which pits principals against teachers in
confrontation situations. The 250 participants
were divided into small groups and the Nominal
Group Technique (NGT) was used to identify the
five most critical administrator/teacher relations
problems facing them personally. Also, possible
solutions to these problems were discussed in the
25 small groups.

The five most critical problems were
identified as: 1) collective bargaining including
negotiations, unionism, and labor vs. management;
2) teacher evaluation/supervision vs. evaluation;
3) lack of mutual trust between administrators
and teachers; 4) lack of accurate and current
information/poor communications; and 5) soured
teacher and administrator attitudes toward life
and work. Most educators and sociologists see
the root cause of most administrator/teacher
relations problems as a lack of communication
and human trust and that collective bargaining
or other political encounters are mere symptoms
of problems lying deep within people who make up
school organizations.

The administrators attending this University
of Akron workshop offered some possible solutions
to better relations between administrators and
teachers. These included: 1) showing a genuine
interest in teachers; 2) keeping teachers well
informed; 3) involving teachers in almost all
decisions/policy making; 4) giving more teacher
recognition when it is due and 5) using staff
meetings for problem solving. Underlying the
solution is the factor of being humanistic in

84

administrator/teacher relationships. The Nominal
Group Technique has proved to be one of the best
methods of encouraging administrators and teachers
to view themselves as part of the problems and
solutions.

IS TEACHING HAZARDOUS TO YOUR HEALTH?

Landsmann, Leanna. Today's Education, Volume 67,
    April-May 1978, pp. 48-50.

    Landsmann reports on a nationwide survey to
focus attention on the health problems of teachers
and the causes of these problems. Instructor,
a magazine for elementary teachers, published a
questionnaire with the cooperation of the American
School Health Association to find out more about
teacher health. This questionnaire contained
two types of questions, those requiring a yes/no
response or one word answer and those requiring
a sentence or short paragraph for an adequate
response. More than 9,000 teachers responded to
the questionnaire, and 98 percent completed all
questions.

    The results of the survey indicated that
eighty-four percent of teachers responding believe
there are health hazards in teaching. The questions that elicited open-ended answers isolated
three major areas of health concern: (1) stress,
(2) weight, diet, and exercise, and (3) physical
environment. Teachers named stress as the major
factor affecting their health. The tension arose
from predictable sources such as discipline
problems, more public pressure on teachers, large
class sizes, and schedules that permit few breaks
or none. The teachers' next most important
health concerns were maintaining proper weight,
achieving proper nutrition, and getting enough
exercise. The results show that more than one-
third of those responding feel that the physical
environment of the school negatively affects
their health. Comments concerning the environment included temperature control in the classroom,

poor lighting, and injuries caused by students such as biting or scratching.

In addition to questions about health concerns, the respondents were asked, "If you could do one thing to improve the health of you and your colleagues, what would that be?" Teachers strongly stated that principals could do much to improve teacher health because they can influence so many of the causes of health troubles. In spite of the fact that eighty percent of teachers responding to the survey have changed their view of teaching since they began, the outlook is still bright. Many teachers are organizing after-school hobby and exercise programs. Some have written that either in teaching centers or in informal rap sessions they are beginning to share and solve the problems that trouble them through improving their physical and mental conditions.

RECERTIFICATION: TOWARD THE BEST USE OF EXPERIENCE

Long, Madeleine J. Action in Teacher Education,
    Volume 1, Spring-Summer 1979, pp. 41-45.

Long describes a recertification program developed by the Board of Education of the City of New York approximately four years ago when critical shortages in junior and senior high school mathematics and science occurred. The author defines recertification as the formal retraining of experienced teachers from one field or level of specialization to another field. This is one important way of retaining the services of the very best teachers when there is oversupply in certain areas and scarcity in other areas. While thousands of teachers were being laid off as a result of declining pupil enrollments in the elementary grades, the Board of Education acted under New York State Law, Section 2588 to give top priority to these laid off teachers through a recertification process.

86

One concrete result in the New York City
program was the establishment of the Mathematics
Institute for High School Teachers. The program
consists of a refresher course, a review of
fundamentals, mathematics courses, and methods
courses offered in a seven week block and
accompanied by small tutorial sessions. In
order for recertification to work, the author
points out that there must be fundamental cooperation among State Education Departments,
local school districts, unions, and universities.
New models of teacher training have to be designed
and evaluated in order to produce the desired
level of competence. The New York City teachers
have been highly successful,based on factors such
as the courses of study were carefully designed
and individually tailored with the finest university mathematics instructors available for teaching
recertification classes.

Despite some problems, the New York City
program has enabled the system to retain its very
best experienced teachers and secure teachers for
disciplines which have been traditionally under-
staffed. Long forecasts that for school and
divisions of education, recertification holds the
promise of an organic role in inservice education
and reintroduces the emphasis on pedagogy as a
discipline.

CONTROVERSY INVOLVING SELECTION OF SCIENCE AND
HUMANITIES TEXTBOOKS

Reynolds, John C. Education, Volume 99, Spring
1979, pp. 250-256.

Reynolds describes and examines the historical/
contemporary impact of textbooks on the curriculum
and the relationship between controversy and textbooks. Specifically, current science and humanities
textbook selection in the states of West Virginia,
California, Virginia, and Tennessee have become
involved in emotional and controversial issues.
In 24 of the 50 states, the state board of
education selects a list of approved textbooks

leaving some choice to each local school district. In the 26 other states, the school districts choose the textbooks.

Because of the concrete nature of textbooks, the general public can relate to them. These attitudes, feelings, and emotions are sometimes mixed in with the professional selection and utilization of textbooks. In the areas of the biological sciences and the humanities, controversy has arisen over the textbook treatment of creation/ evolution, profanity in books, downgrading of America, communism, the Man: A Course of Study (MACOS) materials, religion, race, drugs, and other controversial topics.

The problem of textbook selection in all 50 states becomes one of how to best provide the most effective text materials for the schools even though controversy and attempts at censorship may arise in some situations. Reynolds believes that the diversity inherent in democratic textbook selection, content, and utilization can insure the most effective input from the various groups concerned with textbooks: the publishers, administrators, school board members, teachers, parents, and students. In each school district across the nation, this calls for a determined and cooperative approach to textbook selection.

FLORIDA'S NEW TEACHER CERTIFICATION LAW

Robinson, Andrew A. and David Mosrie. Phi Delta Kappan, Volume 61, December 1979, pp. 263-264.

Robinson and Mosrie report on Florida's new teacher certification law, State Bill 549, which was passed in 1978 and requires 1) an entry examination for students desiring to enroll in a preservice teacher education program in Florida; 2) a comprehensive written examination prior to initial certification; 3) a year-long internship or three years of successful teaching experience

prior to regular certification; 4) a single type
of teaching certificate regardless of degree
level -- bachelor's, master's, or doctorate; and
5) a five year validity period for certificates.
The implication for this is that colleges of
education in the state are not meeting the needs
of future classroom teachers. This new legislation
shifts the responsibility of recertification from
colleges to local districts.

Although there are many interesting facets
to the law, one of the key ones is that each
school district is required to develop a five
year master plan for inservice education. In
summary, Florida is one of eight states that now
require preservice teachers to pass a competency
test for certification. But, as noted above,
the state of Florida goes even further in mandating
a qualifying exam before teacher training, a year
long internship, and limited validity for teaching
certificates. Whether this new law will prove
workable and successful must await further
evaluation and feedback.

TEACHER BURNOUT: A TEACHER CENTER TACKLES THE
    ISSUE

Sparks, Dennis. Today's Education, Volume 69,
    November-December 1979, pp. 37-39.

Sparks reports on a teacher center which
has tackled the problem of teacher stress and
burnout. The symptoms may include exhaustion,
tension, and various physical ailments. Job
related stress has diminished the satisfaction
that many teachers derive from their work,
has caused some educators to choose alternative
careers, and lessened the energy and creativity
that many teachers bring to their classrooms.

The Northwest Staff Development Center (NSDC),
a federally funded teacher center, developed a
program to address the issue of teacher stress
and burnout. NSDC serves approximately 4,000

teachers and administrators in seven districts in northwest Wayne County, Michigan. This center serves as an outreach and provides programs and services for grades K-12 in more than 100 school buildings in a relatively large geographic area. Findings show many causes for teacher stress and burnout in this area. These included changing student and community attitudes toward education, collective bargaining issues, repeated lay offs of professional staff, poor relationships within the schools, and lack of job mobility. Too frequently these issues have resulted in lowered morale and in apathy toward professional development and school improvement.

Responding to the problem of job related stress, NSDC offered a series of workshops on the theme of Prevention and Management of Educational Stress. The seven workshops in this particular series included Stress and the Classroom Teacher, Stress and the School Administrator, Time Management for Educators, Relaxation Techniques, Human Potential, Group Problem Solving, and Career Change. One underlying assumption for the workshops was that extreme stress was detrimental to teachers and their students but some forms of it can lead to professional growth through a thorough examination of stress causes. The workshop entitled Stress and the Classroom Teacher was the most comprehensive of the seven and it served as a starting point for other workshops in the series. This workshop defined four goals: 1) to reduce the isolation, 2) to identify the sources of job related stress, 3) to identify professional strengths and successful work experiences that participants can draw on to increase their satisfaction with teaching, and 4) to form a plan to prevent or ease distress.

Sparks sees the workshops as concrete expressions of inservice programs based on teacher needs. He recognizes that no single, simple solution to school distress exists, that the interactive approach encourages curriculum change when needed, and that teachers who

participate acquire techniques which they can use
to help themselves and distressed students in
their classrooms.

THE EXPANDING ROLE OF TEACHERS IN NEGOTIATING
   CURRICULUM

Vaughn, Jacequeline B.   Educational Leadership,
      Volume 34, August 1977, pp. 21-23.

      Vaughn reports that teachers should and are
seeking a greater role in curriculum decision
making through collective bargaining and outlines
the process and provisions that teachers in
Chicago have been able to negotiate. The author,
who is vice president of the Chicago Teachers
Union, stresses the fact that publishers,
communities, and students have had a great input
into curriculum decisions but that teachers, as
agents of implementation, have been denied the
opportunity to participate. With the advent of
accountability, it seems logical that teacher
unions would seek a greater voice into the
systems of goals and objectives for which the
teachers are directly responsible.

      Through collective bargaining, the position
that curriculum matters are outside the influence
of the union has been changed and is reflected in
a current agreement between the Chicago Board of
Education and the Chicago Teachers Union which
demands classroom teachers equal representation
on all curriculum writing and evaluating committees
in all subjects and textbook selections. As an
extension of benefits, this contract also insures
the same yearly rate of salary for participation.
Other areas of agreement are: curriculum guides to
be provided for and used by all teachers;
extensive use of curriculum texts and supplementary
materials; joint participation in the formation
of quality programs for inner city schools,
involvement of principal, staff, pupils, and school
community in discussion of curriculum objectives;
and principal-staff planning periods for the
development of instruction.

According to Vaughn, it is through the collective voice of one teacher organization officially designated as the bargaining agent that relevant goals can be developed and changes in curriculum and programs be negotiated. It is realized that the most effective programs will be developed through the joint participation of administration, students, teachers, local and state boards, together with local, state, and federal government agencies. However, quotas of representation will not always insure quality educational programs through curriculum development. It is equally important for bargaining to insure competency, knowledge, and experience in developing the curriculum.

Other References

Bridge, Jacque T., Claude H. Cunningham, and Janet Forsbach. "Faculty Stability and Effective Schools," National Association of Secondary School Principals Bulletin, Volume 62, April 1978, pp. 36-41.

Clayton, Marian S. "Religious Cults: What Should Teachers Know and Do About Them?", Today's Education, Volume 68, September - October 1979, pp. 74-76.

Duke, Daniel L., Robert Donmoyer, and Greg Farman. "Emerging Legal Issues Related to Classroom Management," Phi Delta Kappan, Volume 60, December 1978, pp. 305-309.

Dunlap, John F. "California's Chicken-or-Egg Question: Statewide Union or Statewide Bargaining First?", Phi Delta Kappan, Volume 59, March 1978, pp. 458-461.

Freeman, Jayne. "The Joy of Teaching: Another Case History," Phi Delta Kappan, Volume 61, December 1979, pp. 254-256.

Freiwald, J. Leo. "Tenure: Another Sacred Cow About to Bite the Dust?", Phi Delta Kappan, Volume 61, September 1979, p. 50.

Hickey, M. E. "Putting Closed Schools to Good Use," The American School Board Journal, Volume 146, February 1979, pp. 28-29.

Kerman, Sam. "Teacher Expectations and Student Achievement," Phi Delta Kappan, Volume 60, June 1979, pp. 716-718.

Kowalski, Theodore J. and Michael P. Benway. "Dismissal for Immorality," National Association of Secondary School Principals Bulletin, Volume 63, April 1979, pp. 76-82.

Lieberman, Myron. "Eggs That I Have Laid: Teacher Bargaining Reconsidered," Phi Delta Kappan, Volume 60, February 1979, pp. 415-419.

LoPresti, Peter L. "California: The Impact of the Commission for Teacher Preparation and Licensing," Phi Delta Kappan, Volume 58, May 1977, p. 674-677.

Maxson, Marilyn H. and Larry L. Kraus. "Curriculum Censorship in the Public Schools," The Educational Forum, Volume 43, May 1979, pp. 393-407.

Miller, Dean F. and Jan Wiltse. "Mental Health and the Teacher," Journal of School Health, Volume 44, September 1979, pp. 374-377.

Munnelly, Robert J. "Dismissal for Professional Incompetence," Contemporary Education, Volume 50, Summer 1979, pp. 221-225.

Pharis, William L. "Bucks, Benefits, and Bargaining: The Big Picture," National Elementary Principal, Volume 57, March 1978, pp. 22-27.

Sinowitz, Betty E. "The Teacher and the Law: Association Activity Rights," Today's Education, Volume 67, April-May 1978, pp. 20-21.

Small, Robert C., Jr. "Censorship, Schools, and Textbooks," Kappa Delta Pi Record, Volume 13, April 1977, pp. 125-127.

Wallace, James M. "The Making of a Profession: An Oregon Case Study," Phi Delta Kappan, Volume 58, May 1977, pp. 671-673.

Walsh, Debbie. "Classroom Stress and Teacher Burnout," Phi Delta Kappan, Volume 61, December 1979, p. 253.

White, Eileen. "Should School Systems Pull Out of Social Security?", The American School Board Journal, Volume CLVI, November 1979, pp. 25-29.

Zettel, Jeffrey J. and Frederick J. Weintraub.
    "PL94-142: Its Origins and Implications,"
    National Elementary Principal, Volume 58,
    October 1978, pp. 10-13.

CHAPTER V

INVOLVEMENT

There was a time when all of the major civic, social, and educational activities of a community took place in one of two structures, the school or the church. The prominence of both of these sites has decreased significantly during the last two decades. In the case of school, the increased size of districts along with related expansion of bureaucratic structures within the systems have been responsible for much of this change. The size changes were often results of consolidation of schools which frequently meant mergers between rural and suburban areas or several rural communities. In order to provide the greatest economic efficiency and program structure, many smaller schools serving junior high or high school students were closed to permit larger, comprehensive facilities and programs to be established. This more generally offered expanded curricular and socialization opportunities for the students, but it also reduced parental and community involvement in programs since the "community school" concept had been lost.

To balance out consolidation, there has been a significant expansion in recent years of community colleges, junior colleges, decentralization approaches, parental involvement, and an emphasis on neighborhood schools. Many career education programs, community services, volunteer programs, and adjunct teaching resource activities are planned and implemented within the existing school structure.

The last five years have included federal, state, and local efforts to enhance student, parent, and community involvement in school programs and policies. Community colleges have expanded their programs through both credit and non-credit studies designed to meet the needs of the life-long learners.

96

Such activities as comprehensive needs assessment
and referendums have renewed parental and community
concern regarding programs of school systems.
Parent groups also have been formed to support the
school and provide parent educational programs.
At the same time there has been adverse criticism
of schooling and caustic efforts to limit educational
finance. Legislation passed by popular demand in
some states to limit taxation for education has
curtailed efforts to improve education and in some
ways negatively influenced the curriculum. The
cuts in most cases have been applied to the arts
and the psychological and human relations resource
personnel. Taxpayers who flocked to the polls to
support Proposition 13 and similar spin-off
legislation in other states are beginning to take
a more serious look at what these stringent movements are doing to the education of youth.

The school's role in this changing society has
become one of guiding students toward those skills
which are essential to the problem solving process.
Emphasis is being placed on matching the curriculum
to the learning style of each individual student.
Many career education programs specifically
designed for community input are attempting to
meet these individual and varied needs.

The schools have undergone various changes as
a result of the emphasis on student rights and
input. Many of the innovative programs have not
proved successful because of a lack of parental
or faculty support. This has shown the importance
of having a philosophical base as a foundation
for development of a broad achievable educational
goal in a school system. It is necessary that
each element of the educational community, staff
members, parents, and students take part in the
development of this philosophical base and be aware
of the broad parameters within which the school
is to function.

It is now being recognized that the school as
an institution cannot legally prevent students

from obtaining an education which is personally satisfying and socially meaningful. The student has a right to be a part of decision making. By placing the student in a well-planned system of behavioral objectives and performance assessment, teachers and administrators may have more control over the student than they have had before.

Many programs are being designed to assist parents in working with their children in building readiness for schooling and assisting children in carrying on their school work. Such programs usually result in better adjustment and academic achievement of children and increased support of parents for schools. This is particularly true when parent education programs are designed to meet multicultural needs.

The school has the responsibility to give students freedom to practice behavior that is expected of adults in a democratic society. The lowering of the age of legal citizenship of youth is making it more difficult for the school to tell the student what to do. The student, however, still needs assistance in making choices in accordance with his interests. The degree of successful reform is determined by the educational establishment's ability to change its attitudes toward people. Since the principal has direct contact with all levels of the educational hierarchy, participative rather than autocratic leadership on his part can cause a school to be more relevant and improve the learning climate.

When students, faculty, and community are involved in decision-making and program implementation, teachers assume a new form of leadership. They relate to students from a posture of respect. They learn to appreciate diversity, become energetically accountable, negotiate honestly, recognize that some conflicts are irreconcilable, and view rules in the context of the desired ends. Accordingly, new relations are established between the school and the outside world.

Where parent education programs have involved more than one community in working together, they have changed for the better the perceptions of the various groups among themselves and among the school. Pertinent examples are the parents-as-partners approach and magnet schools designed for excellence in a specified area.

Desegregation has taken place much more smoothly when the school people worked to bring the various ethnic groups together for common purposes and involved them in setting goals for education of their children. Magnet schools designed to provide a specialized program in specific areas with admission of the races according to quotas were particularly successful in the Dallas and Houston areas. The peer group encounter process used in weekend retreats has also proved successful in bringing order to some racially torn communities. Community learning programs involving businesses in the work experience aspect of education gave support to educational programs and gained increased and improved resources for all concerned.

A valuable task being utilized in community development is the local school-community advisory council, designed to bridge gaps and ease community tension. All types of school and community problems can be dealt with at the council level including busing, boundary changes, discipline, ethnic differences, and curriculum modifications.

The consideration of community services in the areas of environmental renewal, drug education, career education, and volunteer assistance have contributed to a stronger commitment to solving community problems. A community and school entering a program usually work within the existing framework of the school and the funds provided. An effort to achieve maximum participation is a key factor in developing a community oriented program.

In many places, parents serve on advisory councils, work as volunteers in the schools and in developmental curriculum activities, and serve as resource persons in specialized content areas. Many of the volunteer programs are staffed by parents who assist with playground, cafeteria, or clerical duties. Parental advisory groups are made aware of the laws and policies of their school district and are expected to operate within legal authority. It has been found that when neighborhood residents have been permitted to function as classroom aides, resource persons, and volunteers in a variety of school activities such as remedial tutors under close supervision, their feeling of self-worth has improved, and they have served as effective liaison persons in improved communication between the school and the community.

There has been a recent emphasis on community-centered schools. Big is not always necessarily better. Some small community schools have programs of studies which assist students in making career choices. Community schools tend to focus on the relevant concerns of students and the community at large. Many of these school/community partnerships are being developed from urban to suburban and rural locations. Location is not as important as the prevailing attitude that the school/community partnership can produce useful curriculum programs for the young people of the community.

Many situations show that community/school programs are characterized by intensive involvement, learner-centered schools, resource persons, multi-age grouping, individualized instruction, success oriented programs, cooperative decision-making, out-of-school learning, a community philosophy, and modified buildings. These characteristics seem to emerge wherever a successful school/community program is established. Parents, through many varied programs working closely with faculty supervision, are becoming more involved through school-oriented educational programs. Common outcomes of the programs are the strengthening of the family as a unit and the complementary influence of home, school, and community on the student.

Students, faculty, school administrators, and the community work with and share commitment, control, and involvement in many school systems around the nation. Community education then is a new form that mobilizes heretofore untouched physical and human resources for educational, cultural, and social growth. Thus, it has been found that the greater role the parents play in policy making of the school, the smoother the operation of the school becomes.

The education profession is recognizing that parents are the backbone of successful education, are including them in decision making, and are utilizing their talents and service as para-professionals in many ways. Student participation has been on the increase across the country in determining what is pertinent to their needs. Faculty and administrative assistance have been provided in the school/community programs in many and varied ways.

Where there are opportunities to participate and choose, conflict is minimized. As offerings and programs prove successful, more support is provided in that direction.

Learning about the skills involved in group processes, committee activities, and the give and take of negotiations are important aspects of school/community activities. These skills are improved as the school/community content areas are strengthened through the participation of various resources persons and groups who bring an expertise which is unique to the content programs of the community. In this climate education becomes process oriented and adaptable to the changes of society, thereby rendering education relevant to the individual needs of youth.

COMMUNITY CONTROL THAT SUCCEEDED

Brown, Frank. Educational Forum, Volume 42, May
 1978, pp. 451-457.

Brown presents information about a successful
community controlled school that has succeeded for
nine years. Inner city residents of Buffalo,
frustrated by the failure of local authorities to
integrate the public schools, began to demand
control of neighborhood schools as an alternative
to racial integration. Today, the Buffalo
experiment, which started in 1969, is still in
operation and is considered a success by teachers,
administrators, and parents.

The BUILD Academy in Buffalo, New York, began
with a campaign to end segregation of schools in
Buffalo. While talks were in progress between
BUILD and the Buffalo Board of Education about
school integration, the parents felt that the
board showed a lack of sensitivity to the community
in making decisions. With assistance from a local
civil rights group, the parents and students
boycotted the school, and subsequent negotiations
with the board of education resulted in a Community
Advisory Board to make policies for the school.
The Board of Education, however, retained veto
power over all decisions made by the school
advisory board.

According to Brown, this experiment suggests
that individual school governance within large
school districts can work and that: 1) parents
can handle decision-making power about curricula
and personnel matters, 2) the school is a better
place for children to be educated if their parents
are involved meaningfully, 3) black parents are
very interested in the education for their children,
and 4) professionals can find satisfaction in
working within community controlled schools.

EDUCATING YOUR CHILD AT HOME: THE PERCHEMLIDES
CASE

Bumstead, Richard A. Phi Delta Kappan, Volume 61,
October 1979, pp. 97-100.

The author illustrates the problems and
issues involved when parents attempt to educate
their children at home. He outlines the legal
case of the Perchemlides family versus Donald
Frizzle, the superintendent of schools in Amherst,
Massachusetts.

Bumstead cites Frizzle's initial reasons for
rejecting the Perchemlides curriculum as lack of
training or background of the parents, lack of
sequencing and skill development in the plan, and
absence of opportunity for group experience. The
author notes that whereas lack of equivalency was
the official reason for rejection, other factors
such as bad precedent, questions regarding the
parents' motives, and misgivings regarding monitoring of the plan were also present.

The author presents Justice John Greaney's
comments in maintaining that parents must be
allowed to decide whether public education, including its socialization aspects, is desirable or
undesirable. Judge Greaney identified five factors
that should be considered: 1) the competence of
the teachers; 2) the teaching of subjects required
by law or regulation; 3) the manner in which the
subjects are taught so as to impart knowledge
comparable as given in the local schools; 4) the
number of hours and days devoted to teaching; and
5) the availability of periodic tests and measurements of the child's educational growth.

Bumstead states that the Perchemlides curriculum was approved following Judge Greaney's decision
but that as of August 1979 the case had not been
closed. However, since the fundamental issues
were joined, Perchemlides v. Frizzle expands and
informs the case law supporting the right to
educate at home.

SURVIVAL READING FOR PARENTS AND KIDS: A PARENT
   EDUCATION PROGRAM

Cassidy, Jack and Carol Vukelich.   The Reading
    Teacher, Volume 31, March 1978, pp. 638-641.

    Cassidy and Vukelich reported a series of
workshops in the Newark, Delaware, area designed
so that parents could help their children with
functional or survival reading (reading designed
to help with daily aspects of life such as
recognizing names of street signs, reading recipes,
labels, applications, and contracts).   The school
district offered five workshops on functional
reading skills for parents of primary grade
children (ages five through seven).   The workshops
were conducted by elementary reading specialists
and elementary preservice teachers interested in
reading.   The objectives of the workshops were for
parents to make games that could be used to
reinforce functional reading skills - games
utilizing words and materials in the daily lives
of the children.   Parents gave their children a
"pretest" in order to determine on which level to
construct the materials.

    The workshops proved beneficial in many ways.
Parents were able to realize the importance of the
materials; they did not feel threatened by lack
of knowledge of reading skills; and the workshops
were a means of communication between parents and
workshop presenters.   Parents said that their
children enjoyed the games and activities they
had made.   Although there were some problems
associated with attendance, more children bene-
fitted from the materials than was indicated by
attendance of parents at the workshops.   It was
reported in one instance that even though only
eight parents went to the workshop, 40 children
were able to use the games.

104

ESTABLISHING A PARENT EDUCATION RESOURCE CENTER

Edmister, Patricia. Childhood Education, Volume 54, November-December 1977, pp. 62-66.

In Montgomery County, Maryland parent education classes with a life-cycle approach offered through the Department of Adult Education, Montgomery County Public Schools, are proving to be a source of information and support for parents. Due to the increasing requests for materials, a Parent Education Resource Center has been established. The facility, which was converted from a junior high school classroom, consists of four areas: 1) a children's discovery corner, with activities and materials of interest to preschoolers, allowing parents to bring their young children with them; 2) an adult area with shelves and stands filled with current publications of interest to parents; 3) a multimedia audiovisual equipment area for use in viewing and listening to filmstrips, records, slides, and video tape cassettes; and 4) record and toy lending facility areas.

All printed materials, records, and toys can be borrowed for two weeks with a limit of two books and two records per adult and two books per child. One toy per child may be borrowed with a family limit of three toys. Audiovisual aids may be used for one week.

Resource Center personnel have found that many pamphlets and paperback materials can be obtained at nominal cost through government printing offices. Many other materials are provided free from State and Local Extension Services and Departments of Public Health. Close contact with agencies in the community has proved beneficial in helping the Center obtain materials as well as equipment.

105

THE HAWAII MULTICULTURAL AWARENESS PILOT PROJECT
   (HMAP)

Forman, Sheila and Ron Mitchell. Educational
   Perspectives, Volume 16, December 1977,
   pp. 26-28.

   One of the major multicultural program development efforts undertaken in Hawaii with Emergency
School Aid Act (ESSA) funds is described by Forman
and Mitchell. The Curriculum Research and Development Group of the College of Education of the
University of Hawaii, under contract to the State
Department of Education, is designing and pilot-
testing the Hawaii Multicultural Awareness Pilot
Program (HMAP). Now in its third year of operation,
HMAP is avoiding the "head-on" ethnic studies
program approach that is often used in highly
polarized racial and cultural situations. Instead,
the 12-16 week program being developed for upper-
elementary, intermediate, and high school levels
has organizing themes built around certain
cultural universals in order to illuminate the
multicultural realities in Hawaii. Examples include
life-style and community celebrations (4th grade),
school communities (6th grade), and modern Hawaii
(high school).

   Other design characteristics of the program
include the interweaving of multicultural living
in Hawaii themes, cross-cultural student interaction
and activities, and individualization and person-
alization of learning. Further characteristics
central to the programs are localization of program
materials, maximum utilization of community resource
persons and multilingual access with the translation
of program materials into the various languages
represented among those groups presently immigrating
to Hawaii.

   Preliminary evaluation data on tested programs
indicate a very positive reception of HMAP materials
and activities by students, teachers, and principals.
Work is still in progress to obtain suitable summa-

tive evaluation criteria to measure the substantive
goals and objectives of the program.

GATEWAY TO GROWTH: ST. LOUIS ADVENTURE

Gautier, Marjorie Jane, Nancy Brown, and William
     A. Raisch. Educational Leadership, Volume 35,
     February 1978, pp. 384-389.

During the spring of 1977, a curriculum
improvement project was put into effect at East
Ladue Junior High School in suburban St. Louis,
involving the cooperative efforts of teachers,
counselors, administrators, parents and other
community members. Four central city neighborhoods
for student exploration were preselected on the
basis of: common elements for comparison and/or
contrast, possibility of one day coverage, presence
of receptive contacts for students, diversity within the neighborhood, acceptability to parents, and
accessibility by public transportation.

After several class activities oriented toward
a general stimulation of student interest in and
involvement with the city, its history, its people,
its problems, and its offerings, students were
engaged in firsthand observation of four neighborhoods. Based upon expressed interest in a particular neighborhood, students divided into groups of
four to six to share the tasks necessary for
planning their groups' excursions. Upon completing
their planned activities in their chosen neighborhoods, each group shared its experiences with the
others in the classroom in a variety of follow up
activities.

Results of pre-test post-test measurement of
student perceptions of life in the city indicated
a change in student thinking toward more realistic
perceptions. According to the authors, the program
provided a new stimulus to learning for almost all
those involved in it. Future plans call for the
St. Louis Adventure to be more interdisciplinary.

107

CONTRACTING WITH PARENTS

Lewis, Ronald H. Middle School Journal, Volume 10,
   November 1979, pp. 4, 30.

Lewis presents an approach for instituting a
contract which demonstrates a commitment to the
concept of shared accountability as developed in
the schools of Plainfield, New Jersey when the
school district spent two years developing its
statement of responsibilities. The educators
worked with parents in development of a statement
of parent responsibilities. A third element, the
role of religious institutions, was the concern of
local ministers who committed themselves to total
support of parents and teachers.

A Parent-as-Partner Contract was developed by
parents and teachers. The parents were encouraged
to sign contracts at Back-to-School Night in
September or submit them by mail. Some of the
contract statements of parents were to see that the
child gets to school on time, to see that the child
has some quiet time for homework each evening with
television turned off, to encourage and listen to
an account of the child's day at school. The
teachers' part of the contract included, among
other things, efforts to maintain communication
with parents, raise students' levels of achievement,
and notify parents and students of grading and
homework policies.

The district test scores, as measured by
New Jersey's statewide test and the Metropolitan
Achievement Test, have shown a substantial increase
in reading and math for the past three years since
the contracts have been in effect. Lewis concludes
that this positive trend indicates that statements
of responsibility by schools, parents, and church
can be meaningful and can cause the students to
learn better.

THE CARTERET STORY: THE PEER GROUP DEALS WITH
   RACIAL CONFLICTS

Liss, Moe and James C. Robinson.   Phi Delta Kappan,
   Volume 60, November 1978, pp. 169-172.

   Liss and Robinson give an account of the change
that took place in the racially torn school community of Carteret, New Jersey. After severe violence
causing closing of schools, the board of education
took strategic steps to deal with the conflict.
Among these were the establishment of committees
whereby peer group encounter processes could
function. The highlight of this process came
about through a well-planned weekend retreat of
selected students.

   Fifty students and eight faculty members were
involved in a Human Relations Peer Group Leadership
Training Program. The students were selected
according to their knowledge, involvement, and
leadership in the dissident groups. The process
involved a four-day intensive training program
conducted by the Center for Organization and
Personal Effectiveness (COPE). It was designed
to provide training in racial-ethnic awareness and
understanding, interpersonal communication, and
shared problem-solving while at the same time
creating a closed environment within which students
would be required to interact. Students were
involved in recognizing and examining blockages to
racial-ethnic harmony that they had had a part in
perpetuating.

   Moving from an atmosphere of tense hostility,
students at the retreat were guided in expressing
their feelings and facing the issues involved,
while working and engaging in recreation together.
The outcome was the development of plans for
improving school relations which included students
taking the leadership in policing their school with
the removal of outside police.

   According to Liss and Robinson, the program
proved to be successful in bringing new awareness

among both students and faculty, opening communication between the racial and ethnic groups,
resolving immediate conflicts between participating
students, and developing and implementing a plan of
action which brought about harmony in the school.

CENSORSHIP AND THE SCHOOLS: A DIFFERENT PERSPECTIVE

Mour, Stanley I. English Journal, Volume 66,
     February 1977, pp. 18-20.

        In 1973, the Supreme Court of the United States
affirmed a prior opinion that obscene materials are
not protected by the First Amendment. Mour reports
on a year-long effort by the Jefferson County,
Kentucky, Commission on Community Standards Relating
to Obscenity to respond to this affirmation. The
commission was composed of eighteen individuals
representing a cross-section of the community with
respect to sex, age, occupation, level of education,
political affiliation, and religious preference.
The commission was given four objectives. The
author focuses his attention upon one of these,
that the commission should "seek information and
insights regarding 'contemporary standards' if
such exist in Jefferson County."

        The Commission worked for a year beginning in
October, 1973, soliciting position statements from
the community, listening to experts in particular
areas relating to the topic, reading pertinent
documents, studying legal decisions and ordinances,
and holding four public hearings. Mour states that
the results of the work were enlightening but that
what the Commission failed to do was just as
enlightening and important.

        No concrete guidelines were established to
determine what is and is not obscene in the county.
The Commissioners were unable to reach consensus on
a definition of obscenity or community, and obscenity
itself was viewed as a problem by only a small
albeit vocal portion of the population. Less than

10% of the questionnaires designed to elicit
community feelings were returned and attendance
at public meetings was low. The author states that
concern over obscenity in Jefferson county seemed
related to socio-economic level and political
persuasion. Persons from depressed and upper
socio-economic classes were less concerned about
obscenity than persons from the working/middle
classes. Persons vocalizing belief that obscenity
was a serious problem tended to be "right-of-
middle" along a political continuum.

Mour concludes by offering four specific
steps that schools and school personnel should
take to defuse controversial issues: 1) school
personnel should become well acquainted with the
standards and ethics of their communities; 2) each
school should establish an advisory committee to
evaluate and select materials; 3) explicit procedures for grievances should be established; and
4) the school and district should continually
communicate information concerning materials to
its patrons.

WHEN THE COMMUNITY BECOMES THE TEACHING GROUND

Naumann, Joseph A., Jr. Educational Leadership,
    Volume 37, January 1980, pp. 332-333.

The author describes the Community Learning
Program operating at McCluer North Senior High
School in Florissant, Missouri. Through work
study programs students are exposed to the widest
possible range of skills and professions in the
area. They spend three class periods per day,
four days a week for nine weeks, with business
and professional sponsors supplementing the working
experience in school discussions and study projects.
Some of the fields to which they are exposed are
accounting, fire fighting, law, nursing, teaching,
and x-ray technology. Journals kept by the students
are reviewed regularly by the faculty advisors.

Naumann reports many positive results including increased confidence on the part of students in themselves and their abilities, better ability to communicate with others, and practical training which led to better job opportunities and employment. Furthermore, students received endorsement from business leaders when applying to colleges or vocational schools.

Naumann also states that in response to a survey, sixty percent of the sponsors found students to be more responsible or reliable than they had originally believed. Seventy-nine percent of the respondents reported that they felt more than compensated for any inconvenience they may have been caused, and would recommend participation to other business leaders. Additionally, nearly seventy five percent of the parents questioned said that their children appeared to have a better sense of what they wanted to do after high school.

AN ELEMENTARY SCHOOL WITH PARENTS AND INFANTS

Packer, Athol B., Michael B. Resnick, Jacqueline L. Resnick, and Jennet M. Wilson. Young Children, Volume 34, January 1979, pp. 4-9.

The authors describe a model parenting education program at Prairie View Elementary School in Gainesville, Florida, serving about eighty families with children from birth to age three. The program deals with the parents and their children through sequential classes at four stages of the infants' development: birth to six months, six to twelve months, twelve to twenty-four months, and twenty-four to thirty-six months in age. The classes are conducted by an interdisciplinary team of professionals from child development, early childhood education, maternity-infant nursing, and counseling psychology working with a community home coordinator. Four basic activities are stressed in each class, including exercises and learning activities for the children,

postnatal conditioning and relaxing exercises for
the mothers, a sharing-discussion period, and
interdisciplinary consultation with professional
resource persons.

In addition to the class activities at Prairie
View, the Alachua County Schools maintain a
parenting education program which features a parent
advisory council, a toy lending library, home
visitations, and referral services. Packer,
Resnick, Resnick, and Wilson cite data from the
first year of the program which indicate that
parents were able to handle stressful or
frustrating situations significantly better at
the end of their first year of participation in
the program than they had been when they began
the program eight or nine months earlier.

THIS SCHOOL BOARD LEARNED SEVEN LESSONS IN
    COMMUNITY RELATIONS -- AFTER IT GOT SACKED

Parker, Barbara. American School Board Journal,
    Volume 165, July 1978, pp. 30-32.

Parker examines some of the factors that
resulted in the unprecedented recall of an entire
school board in LaCrosse, Wisconsin. Although the
reasons for the board's dismissal are not completely
clear, the lessons to be learned from the board's
experience are clear, and Parker discusses seven
lessons that any astute school board would be wise
to heed.

The incident that apparently sparked the
recall of the board was their firing of a high
school principal who used "unorthodox" methods to
maintain discipline. The LaCrosse community,
especially the older citizens, approved of the
principal's methods, and disgruntled citizens
angrily demanded his reinstatement and the board's
recall when he was fired. According to one board
member who was recalled, the media "trumped up
discipline problems in LaCross that didn't
exist." Such gross exaggeration of the discipline

113

problem instilled an unwarranted fear in many citizens, and consequently, their wholehearted endorsement of the principal.

Lesson number one, then, according to Parker, is that a school board should not expect the media to be on its side, especially if the board is not supplied with factual evidence.

Second, a wise school board should learn from the LaCrosse coup that the older citizens in a community have a right to know what is going on. A board should never forget to listen to the electorate, and in fact, should seek constantly to communicate effectively with the community. Parker warns board members to constantly bear in mind the fact that being a school board member is a difficult task and that one should never underestimate the power of public opinion.

School officials in LaCrosse have provided a checklist that, if followed, should prevent the problems that resulted in the LaCrosse coup. The six-point checklist suggests that a student conduct code should be established and stresses especially the importance of effective communication with the public and community involvement.

CAL COMMUNITY SCHOOL - SMALL, RURAL AND GOOD!

Skenes, Robert E. and Carolyn Carlyle. Phi Delta Kappan, Volume 60, April 1979, pp. 589-593.

A small but highly successful school district in Iowa is locked in a struggle for survival with the Iowa State Department of Public Instruction (DPI). Skenes and Carlyle report on the CAL (Coulter, Alexander, and Latimer) Community School District's efforts to fight consolidation and state bureaucracy in order to maintain their independent 305 student K-12 system. Iowa's DPI, according to Skenes and Carlyle, insists that "small schools cannot be good schools, because they cannot meet the educational needs of the children." The criterion for meeting these needs appears to be based upon a cost-effectiveness factor rather than more valid indices of a good school such as student attendance, dropout rate, performance as indicated by standardized tests and teacher evaluation, and graduates' performance in higher education or in employment. Viewed in terms of these latter indices, the authors maintain that CAL is highly successful in educating children.

Perhaps the most important factor in CAL's success is the leadership provided by the superintendent. Having been educated in one of Iowa's rural schools, he is appreciative of their strengths such as individual attention given to the students and opportunity for students to participate in many extra-curricular activities. The superintendent places great emphasis upon finding out what the people of the district want and helping them get it, contributing to another factor - community support.

Skenes and Carlyle report that the people in the CAL district strongly support the school, its programs, and teachers. This is observable through school visitations, attendance at parent-teacher conferences and school functions, and marches on the state capitol in response to legislative action which could have meant the loss of their school through consolidation.

Those CAL graduates who go to college do well, and those who settle in the community are recognized as good citizens. Skenes and Carlyle attribute the students' success to the personal approach taken by CAL's teachers -- their emphasis on basic skills and CAL's belief in decentralization. Students treated with respect, the authors contend, benefit from a community school that utilizes all its resources - students, parents, teachers, and administrators.

PARENT EDUCATION PROGRAMS: WHAT DETERMINES
    EFFECTIVENESS?

Stevens, Joseph H., Jr. Young Children, Volume 33,
    May 1978, pp. 59-64.

Stevens reviews the results of research
pertaining to the effectiveness of parent
education programs which are intended to enhance
the parents' role as teachers. Programs such as
Head Start and Follow Through have utilized a
variety of parent involvement and parent education strategies. Parent consultants, teachers,
supervisors, and project directors have been the
groups primarily involved. The participants have
generally been volunteers.

The author states that those programs
especially effective in producing substantial
changes in children's functioning and parental
behavior have worked with parents for a minimum
of 18 to 24 months. Long-term consultation,
which changed in keeping with increased competence
of parent and child, appeared to be of critical
importance for substantial and sustained change.
Stevens notes that other projects utilizing
individual consultation models have provided
the most promising data regarding the continuing
significant effects of such programs.

Stevens reports that some programs may have
detrimental effect on parents' and children's
behavior. One study revealed that one home
treatment group with little supervision and
unfocused treatment efforts produced negative
changes in children's functioning. The author
cautions that programs need to be carefully
conceived, judiciously monitored and evaluated,
and planned in accordance with relevant theory
and research data.

Stevens states that changes in child and
parent behavior produced by effective programs
have occurred in the areas of maternal teaching

116

style and attitude and in children's intelligence, language development, and exploratory behavior. At least one program, the Houston Parent Child Development Center, has incorporated systematic activities for fathers.

Stevens suggests that the effectiveness of a parent education strategy will need validation by replication in various settings to provide answers to several questions. Three areas for future research are identified: the long-term effects of programs upon variables such as the parents' teaching/interactional style and parents' awareness of the role the home environment plays in providing continuing developmental activities; the impact of programs upon the family as a system including possible role relationships between parents; and the examination of the effectiveness of alternative systems for enhancing the parent's skill as a teacher.

PRIME TIME FOR COMMUNICATION

Wilhelms, Fred T. Educational Leadership, Volume 37, November 1979, pp. 171-173.

The author describes the efforts of the Parent Participation TV Workshop sponsored by Teachers Guides to Television to promote dialogue between parents and children about the things that really matter. Wilhelms states that the Parent Participation TV Workshops were selected as one of the eleven programs that work for the U.S.O.E. Commissioner's conference on "Building Confidence in the Public Schools." He notes that the media and especially NBC have shown great interest in the project and have supplied the schools with free materials.

Wilhelms describes the involvement of different school boards in the workshops. Particular attention is given to the use made of Parent Participation TV Workshops in Georgia under the leadership of the Associate State

117

Superintendent, Lucille Jordon.   Advance workshops
with principals, parent leaders, and guidance
counselors were organized around the film "Sooner
or Later."   This enabled leaders to draw upon
community resource groups to develop communication
among the various education and community groups
and respond to questions and concerns generated
from the viewing audience.   Due to the success of
this venture similar experiences were planned
for use of the films of Eliot Wigginton based
on his "Foxfire" series.   That program is even
moving beyond parent participation toward grand-
parent/parent/student workshops.   In reviewing the
past record of performance, the author views the
Parent Participation TV Workshops as an effective
way to open communication within families.   He
sees open communication as a major need to our
society and views the TV Workshops as "an amazing-
ly good answer to that need."

OTHER REFERENCES

Anderson, Bill. "These Districts Use Pro-Management," The American School Board Journal, Volume 167, March 1980, pp. 22-23, 42.

Brodie, Thomas A. "Cooperation Among These Five School Boards Paid Off for Gifted Kids," The American School Board Journal, Volume 167, February 1980, p. 25.

Brown, Doris M. "Saturday School," Phi Delta Kappan, Volume 58, March 1977, p. 575.

Dunaway, David King and Leonard Charles Beckum. "The Mayor's Influence in Urban School Desegregation," Phi Delta Kappan, Volume 58, March 1977, pp. 553-556.

Earle, Jane. "Se Hable Espanol: The Story of the Chicano Education Project," Today's Education, Volume 66, November-December 1977, pp. 76-77.

Ecker-Racz, L. Laszlo. "Public Schools in the Wake of Proposition 13," Today's Education, Volume 68, April-May 1979, pp. 66-73.

Ecker-Racz, L. Laszlo. "Coping with Proposition 13," Today's Education, Volume 67, September-October 1978, pp. 40-45.

Estes, Nolan. "On Eliminating Institutional Racism," Phi Delta Kappan, Volume 60, December 1978, pp. 302-303.

Guthrie, James W. "Proposition 13 and the Future of California's Schools," Phi Delta Kappan, Volume 60, September 1978, pp. 12-15.

Johnson, Edward E. "The Home-School Partnership Model for Follow Through," Theory Into Practice, Volume 16, February 1977, pp. 35-40.

119

Knight, Dorothy. "A Volunteer Learns Her Lesson," *Tennessee Teacher*, Volume 44, January 1977, pp. 3.

Larkin, Joe. "School Desegregation and Student Suspension," *Education and Urban Society*, Volume 2, August 1979, pp. 485-495.

Little, Wesley and Betty Little. "Bridge to the Past, Wind River Native Culture Program," *Childhood Education*, Volume 54, March 1978, pp. 242-245.

Olmstead, Patricia P., Rodman B. Webb, and William B. Ware. "Teaching Children at Home and School," *Theory Into Practice*, Volume 16, February 1977, pp. 17-21.

Powers, P. Joseph. "Will the Delegates Please Take Their Seats? ... a model UN in the Hague," *Today's Education*, Volume 68, September-October 1979, pp. 78-80.

Shea, Joseph and Stevie Hoffman. "Extending the Curriculum: Home Learning Tasks," *Theory Into Practice*, Volume 16, February 1977, pp. 2-6.

Savage, Tom V. Jr., "Community Involvement in Alchohol Education," *The Clearing House*, Volume 51, March 1978, pp. 349-350.

Taylor, Raymond G., Jr. "A Better Way for a Board of Education to Approach Spending Decisions," *Education*, Volume 100, Spring 1980, pp. 206-208.

Terrill, Marguerite M. "Issue: The Local Property Tax and the American Public Schools," *The Clearing House*, Volume 52, April 1979, pp. 384-387.

Washington, Kenneth R. "Success: A Parent Effectiveness Approach for Developing Urban Children's Self-Concepts," *Young Children*, Volume 32, July 1977, pp. 5-10.

Whitesides, Barbara. "The Brookline Early Education Project," <u>Young Children</u>, Volume 33, January 1978, pp. 64-68.

121

CHAPTER VI

ACCOUNTABILITY AND EVALUATION

The educational community has become accustomed to and acutely attuned to issues related to evaluation and accountability. Movements involving national and state assessment, standardized testing, criterion-referenced tests, reporting, grading, faculty evaluation by students, behavioral objectives, rating scales, and legislation for accountability have become commonplace on the local and national scene. These movements have had a definite impact on curriculum planning, design, implementation, and evaluation.

They have been felt at local levels in terms of demands for numerous program changes, systematic teacher and administrative evaluations, and comprehensive testing programs. State-wide concerns for accountability have resulted in legislation related to minimum competency testing in about two-thirds of the states. The national recognition of evaluation as a primary issue in today's educational practice is most obvious in journal designations as the theme for an entire issue and some professional organizations' decisions to present it in one of their conference themes. Additionally, both state and national legislative bodies and professional organizations are spending time and effort considering the possible passage of truth-in-testing laws to control the testing industry and the relationship of them to evaluation programs. Every teacher, supervisor, or administrator is affected by the increased emphasis placed on evaluation and accountability. Everything from the development of daily lesson plans to decisions related to total curriculum designs and textbook adoptions has been modified significantly since these movements have come to the forefront.

Many educators surmise that the accountability movement was not initiated as a way to improve learning opportunities for children but was started in response to problems rising out of the increasing costs of public education. Charges that education is too costly, too nebulous, has failed too many children, and that nobody is ever held accountable are common complaints about education. Added to these charges comes the legal moves to turn over more power to students for regulating their own behavior. The major concern is that students become more responsible as they exercise their newly found rights.

Accountability advocates argue that specific educational procedures and standards should be developed. Individuals should be assigned to responsibilities for which they are evaluated and if they do not measure up or cannot be, retrained then they should be moved out. On the surface the theory seems sound but the problem comes in implementation. Various methods of implementation have been attempted during the past decade. Many of the accountability advocates have not been public educators, and many teachers are concerned that the overemphasis on this type of measurement promises greater conformity and the diminishment of humaneness, individuality, and creativity in public education. Rating sheets and devices to determine teacher effectiveness have become extensive. Concern is expressed that many items monitored have no relation to successful teaching.

The origin of the structure of many educational accountability programs can be traced to concepts practiced and refined in business and industry. Such management programs as the systems approach, management by objectives, and performance contracting are direct adoptions from the business world. These programs have all had one major impact on educational practices. They have forced systems and individuals to identify and assess their system's goals. No one objects to the concept of accountability, but the expectations or goals attached to an individual accountability program are very sensitive and controversial issues. Consequently, many adoptions of local or statewide accountability programs often experience prolonged debate and extensive validation procedures. In a sense, this has deterred the process, but it has also assured greater credibility for the final program.

The increased concern for education of good quality has brought about increased expenditure, federal involvement, and variety in educational processes. Several plans have surfaced as a result of this accountability movement. Statewide assessment plans are being emphasized which usually establish a series of fairly broad educational goals, then designate means to determine the degree to which students conform to these goals. Using this means teacher evaluation is determined by student achievement scores.

The competency based and performance based programs now in use with teachers, supervising teachers, supervisors, and administrators are pertinent examples of accountability. The promoters of the movement contend that specific measurable skills necessary for teaching and leading can be isolated and taught to prospective instructors and administrators. However, those persons who gain authority to select the competency components gain the decision-making power. It becomes a necessity to have cooperation and input from all involved.

In spite of the accountability movements' discrepancies and disabling factors, educators generally agree that evaluation is central to the whole process of educational change. Since the overall aim of education is the improvement of individual learning, it is important that evaluation include measurement of the extent to which students achieve instructional objectives, continuous feedback data to students and teachers, the effectiveness of teaching in helping students achieve objectives, and the success of educational

125

programs in attaining desired objectives. Instead of certifying that a student has spent so much time in school or taken so many courses, the schools need to be able to certify that a student is able to perform specific tasks, indicating his skills in such areas as reading, writing, computer programming, or automobile mechanics.

A very positive aspect emerging from the accountability/assessment movement is new tests designed to measure what is learned more effectively. Criterion-referenced tests are recommended by many educators as a replacement for norm-referenced tests. These criterion tests are more accurate in their measurement of outcomes because they are geared to what a student learns over a specific period of time. In keeping with this is comprehensive achievement monitoring which affords regular testing activities with tests corrected by computer and returned to the classroom within two days with a printout indicating the percentage of students answering each item correctly, thus becoming a management tool for the teacher.

The increased concern for quality in education and for equality of educational opportunity has brought greatly expanded expenditures for education along with more federal involvement in education. These developments have led to recognition of the need for valid and reliable assessments of the results of our educational efforts. Administrators and teachers are helping young people seek more creative and permanent goals in their efforts to get an education. They are being given the opportunity to achieve usable knowledge about their true abilities to learn. Through this approach more emphasis is being placed on learning and teaching and less on marks.

New materials and methods are being employed that modify the traditional evaluation methods. Technology, computers, and competency materials

are helping to revolutionize evaluation procedures.
Less emphasis is being placed on traditional
grading by the teacher in an effort to give more
time to better preparation for teaching. With
this shift in emphasis, the curriculum is being
designed to allow for qualitative assessment and
maximal individual development with students
being more involved in their own evaluation, thus
furthering the concepts of responsibility. New
means of evaluation are changing the role of the
teacher from judge to evaluator.

Grading systems and means of reporting to
parents are important factors in student assessment.
Parents should bear in mind that accountability
means being held responsible for something over
which one has had direct control. Schools are
directly responsible for the environments which
they create and maintain for children. The
school is responsible for the instruction, but
the parent is responsible for the readiness of
the child to utilize the school environment while
the student is still responsible for the actual
learning. Evaluation of a school is aimed
primarily at how well the environment is arranged
to meet the educational needs of its students.
The school goals, student responses, the learning
environment, student feedback, and current
reporting policies are involved in better understanding marking and reporting. Accountability,
then, is thought of not only as a management
system of checks and balances, but more importantly
as a procedural tool to aid in the process of
making decisions about the instructional efforts
of students, teachers, and the community.
Extensive testing and diagnostic programs are
being used to classify students for all kinds of
special services. The move toward mainstreaming
is now using many evaluative instruments toward
gaining resources in keeping with the needs of
all children.

The call for accountability in education, then,
is a summons to review and reform the educa-

127

tional system. Instead of equating quality in terms of resources allocated through inputs such as teachers, space, and equipment, the criterion is becoming that of results in student learning which may be termed student behavior. A revised educational commitment for the nation becomes every child shall learn, not just that every child will have access to an adequate education.

The rise of the drop-out rate has awakened educators to the fact that children doomed to failure must somehow be rescued and kept in schools that effectively meet their interests and needs. Less attention is being given to grades as the motivator of student learning with more emphasis on the teacher as the motivator, guide, resource person, and aide in student self-evaluation.

State educational accountability acts have attempted to create a manageable assessment system. New minimum graduating standards are being mandated for high school graduates. Objective academic test data along with some efforts to identify proficiency in life role skills are a challenge not only to educators but to society and especially the business man.

The American educational scene is presently witnessing an unprecedented public demand for assessment and accountability of the total public school system. From the basic teacher-made test and the first report card to national assessment, evaluation is a continuous and comprehensive process. Educators are becoming more accountable, are more specific in educational goals, and are utilizing various methods of evaluating student proficiency. This is being accomplished through skills emphasizing the techniques of test construction, a greater utilization of self-testing techniques, a greater comprehension of the relationships between teaching and student achievement, and the development of alternative types of reporting. The measurement of subject area content is being viewed in the total educational picture as an aid to better instruction at all levels. Mastering the skills of assessment and measurement is important to education, students, and the public as a developmental step in accountability. Because of a more expressed need to insure that schools are producing results expected in public education, systematic assessment and accountability procedures are being included in curriculum design and evaluation.

MASTERY LEARNING IN A SMALLER SCHOOL SYSTEM

Abrams, Joan D. Educational Leadership, Volume
37, November 1979, pp. 136-139.

Abrams reports on the approach of mastery
learning instituted in the Red Bank New Jersey
school system as an exciting and viable approach
to improving learning.

The author defines mastery learning as the
identification of topics within a curriculum area
and the development of objectives that test
mastery of each of those topics. Each step used
in the implementation of mastery learning is
described. Basic to this program was the board's
commitment to have every teacher in the school
system participate.

Red Bank teachers were given a minimum of 15
hours of inservice preparation while administrators
and supervisors who would be expected to guide
them were given approximately 30 hours of inservice
preparation. Workshops were videotaped so that
those who missed sessions could arrange for a
showing of the preparations. Each teacher was
expected to prepare a unit to begin teaching for
mastery. While the unit was in operation, the
teacher would prepare another unit, and then
another. Each teacher would have at least one
group in every class engaged in mastery learning.

Abrams discusses three major differences
between mastery learning and traditional teaching -
the most critical being multi-year plans which
require releasing teachers from class for long
periods for planning. The major obstacles to
mastery learning appeared to be time necessary
for inservice training, scheduling for teacher
planning time, and change in teacher attitude.
Some advantages of the program included teacher
realizations of flaws in their presentation of

of materials, reduced teacher threat, pleasure in
achieving goals by both teachers and students,
better organization of materials, decreased
discipline problems, increased motivation and
more positive attitudes toward testing.

Abrams concludes that the Red Bank implementation of mastery learning at this early stage
shows improvement in the basic skills. Even the
children who do not achieve mastery are doing
significantly better than they did under nonmastery
conditions.

AN EVALUATION OF LONG-TERM SSR IN THE JUNIOR HIGH
    SCHOOL

Cline, Ruth K. J. and George J. Kretke. Journal
    of Reading, Volume 23, March 1980, pp. 503-
    506.

Cline and Kretke report a study about junior
high school students in Boulder, Colorado, who
had had three years of SSR (Sustained Silent
Reading); the study compared them with junior high
school students of similar ability and socioeconomic
levels but who had not participated in SSR.

The 111 students in the experimental group had
attended the junior high school with SSR for all
three years. The 138 students in the control
group were composed of students from two junior
high schools with a similar student population but
who had not been exposed to SSR. Students in both
groups were administered a series of standardized
tests during the three year period and an attitude
scale during the last year of the study.

No significant differences were found in
achievement levels between the two groups. The
only significant differences (at the .05 level)
found were in the attitude inventory; there, the
students who had participated in SSR showed a more
positive attitude toward going to the school
library, reading a book of their choice, doing

131

assigned reading as well as expressing a more
positive attitude about the importance of reading
than did the control group.

DIAGNOSING LEARNING STYLES: A PRESCRIPTION FOR
    AVOIDING MALPRACTICE SUITS

Dunn, Rita, Kenneth Dunn, and Gary E. Price. Phi
    Delta Kappan, Volume 58, January 1977, pp.
    418-420.

    The authors describe their Learning Style
Inventory (LSI), a means of determining how
children learn best.   In citing examples of
court cases evidencing the public's demand for
accountability in the public schools, the authors
assert that teachers must determine not only what
a child learns but also why or how he learns.   How
a person learns is probably the most important
factor relating to his academic achievement, yet
few means of making such a diagnosis are available.
The LSI is based on research which indicates that
learners are affected by their: (1) immediate
environment, (2) emotionality, (3) sociological
needs, and (4) physical needs.

    Three times during the spring and summer of
1975, 110 students from grades 3, 4, 7 and 11 in
two middle class school districts participated in
a study to compare their idea of their individual
learning style with their teachers' perception of
how they learn.   Teachers rated each student's
learning style.   The students took the LSI to
provide an indication of each student's learning
style preference.   When comparing teachers' ratings
and students' responses the results indicated that
teachers were aware of certain factors enhancing
learning such as low light, response to adults,
tactile experiences, and kinesthetic experiences.
However, teachers and students disagreed regarding
the students' self-motivation and persistence.

    The authors suggested that 90% of instruction
probably occurs through the lecture method even

though both students and teachers recognized
preferences for learning through tactile or
kinesthetic means supplemented by the visual. Due
to the existence of such discrepancies, parents
could have court cases on the grounds that their
children were prevented from attaining the maximum
potential. However, if teachers diagnose individual learning styles and act accordingly, the public
will be able to see real and measurable results
which will satisfy some parental demands for
accountability.

WHERE EVERYBODY LOVES A TEST

Fedo, Michael W. American Education, Volume 14,
    March 1978, pp. 6-9.

    Fedo describes an achievement monitoring
program in Hopkins, Minnesota where students
regard tests and their computerized scoring system
as a kind of game, while teachers see the system
as a guide to improved teaching. The Comprehensive
Achievement Monitoring (CAM) program has been in
effect in Hopkins, a Minneapolis suburb since 1970.
CAM is based on a project developed at Stanford
University and implemented at the Demonstration
Evaluation Center in Hopkins with the support of
grants under Title II of the Elementary and
Secondary Education Act. CAM promises that:
1) students attending class using the system will
learn more than students not involved in the
program, 2) students will find CAM to be a useful
technique for monitoring their progress in a class,
and 3) teachers using the system will find it eases
the management of classroom instruction.

    A special feature of CAM is a program of
regular testing with tests corrected by computer
and returned to the classroom within 2 days with
a printout indicating the percentage of students
answering each item correctly. CAM thus becomes
a management tool for the teacher.

133

District teachers and CAM professionals work
together to develop course objectives and test
items which are collected by the evaluation center.
The tests are cumulative and are actually three
tests in one - dealing with retention of material
presented, material recently taught, and material
not yet taught. Additionally, a CAM printout every
two weeks serves as a primary vehicle of communication to let the parents and children know what
individual students have accomplished. CAM also
includes some measures related to the effectiveness of teacher presentation of subject matter.

After the initial investment, according to
Fedo, the program costs for each pupil remain low,
only about $5.00 per year. CAM currently serves
more than 12,000 students and 300 teachers in the
Hopkins and neighboring systems. Teachers observe
that constant testing has eliminated the element
of fear from tests. The students are tested so
often, then tend to regard it as fun, a sort of
game.

FLORIDA'S APPROACH TO COMPETENCY TESTING

Fisher, Thomas H. Phi Delta Kappan, Volume 59,
    May 1978, pp. 599-602.

Fisher described the process through which
the Florida accountability system was put into
practice, what it encompasses, and the immediate
effects and results of the testing.

Florida passed its 1976 Educational Accountability Act based on lawmakers and educators'
attempts to create a manageable assessment system.
The act mandates new minimum graduation standards
for the graduating class of 1979. These standards
include mastery of basic skills and satisfactory
performance on a functional literacy test.
Functional literacy was defined as "application
of basic skills to problems encountered in every-
day life." This part of the test included math

134

skills in thirteen categories and eleven categories
of communication skills.

The results included an average failure of
36% on the mathematics section and 8% on the
communication skills section. Students had to
get 70% of the problems correct in order to pass.
The failure for black students was somewhat higher
than that of while students. In some schools with
a large black proportion of students,the failure
rate in mathematics was nearly total. The test
was reviewed for racial bias but none could be
found. Students not passing the test receive
remedial instruction and are retested.

THE COMPETENCY PROGRAM IN NORTH CAROLINA

Gallagher, James J. and Ann Ramsbotham. High
    School Journal, Volume 61, April 1978,
    pp. 302-312.

Gallagher and Ramsbotham discuss the competency program enacted in North Carolina in 1977
designed to provide a continuing picture of North
Carolina students' standing regarding national
norms and to assure that high school graduates
possess minimum competencies. The program,
administered by the Competency Test Commission,
called for trial testing of eleventh grade
students in the spring of 1978 with full scale
testing in the fall of 1978. Remedial instruction
was mandated to assist students with skill
deficiencies. For the trial phase and the first
full scale testing, the Commission recommended
that competencies tested be limited to reading
and mathematics with other areas of competence to
be given future consideration. The focus of the
testing was to be upon ability to apply basic
skills to practical life situations.

The Commission established criteria for
instrument selection and chose three instruments
in each subject area. For the field trial,

approximately one half of the eleventh grade students were scheduled to receive a battery of reading tests plus a reading norm-referenced achievement test from the ninth grade annual test battery. Another group of approximately one half of the students were to encounter a battery of mathematics tests plus a mathematics norm-referenced achievement test from the ninth grade battery. A smaller group of approximately 6,000 students were to respond to one reading and one mathematics competency test in order to establish performance across areas. The information produced by the trial testing was intended to assist in the selection of the best instruments for the Fall 1978 testing.

Gallagher and Ramsbotham identified four issues as crucial determinants of the success of the competency program: 1) the nature of the remediation process, 2) insuring against cultural bias in the testing program, 3) establishment of a cut-off score, and 4) adoption of an alternative to the diploma for students who fail the test.

The authors report that schools across the state were developing remedial programs and cited two specific examples. One high school conducted an after school program to help students not maintaining a C average. The students were volunteers, and individual plans were developed through conferences involving the student, parent, and teacher. Another high school was exploring the establishment of a fundamental skills laboratory providing remedial help during the school day. The Commission had established a special committee to explore the complex issues involved in the question of cultural bias and was examining standard setting procedures across the country to facilitate determination of a cut-off score. Gallagher and Ramsbotham noted that the Commission was moving in the direction of adopting an alternative to the diploma which would provide some indication of a student's level of accomplishment and skills rather than a document which only reflects failure.

AN UP-FRONT APPROACH TO ADMINISTRATIVE EVALUATION

Herman, Jerry J. NASSP Bulletin, Volume 62,
    November 1978, pp. 34-42.

The author describes a tri-fold approach to
administrative evaluation that works for the West
Bloomfield School District, Orchard Lake, Michigan.
The system utilizes a localized version of Management By Objectives (MBO), a comprehensive job
description, and a self-evaluation guide serving
as a discussion tool during evaluation conferences.

Herman states that members of the total
administrative team at building and central office
levels conducted an extensive analysis of management functions in order to create and maintain an
effective management operation. The job descriptions developed by the team were approved by the
board of education and became an integral part of
the evaluation methodology, comprising approximately
50% of the standard of evaluation. One such job
description for the position of senior high
assistant principal for student services covering
17 specific duties and responsibilities is
presented.

Yearly performance objectives, limited to a
maximum of ten, are written for each administrator.
The objectives may evolve from suggestions made
by the administrator being evaluated, other members
of the management team, or from problems identified
from the previous year. These objectives, weighted
in priority order, are designed to be self-correct-
ing and comprise approximately 50% of the standard
of evaluation. Herman includes the three primary
objectives and sub-objectives agreed to for one
principal for one school year.

The author notes that the self-evaluation
guide sheet accomplishes several purposes including
identification of possible objectives for future
years and generation of suggestions for improving
management functions. This guide does not, however,
enter into the final evaluation.

Herman recommends the West Bloomfield plan
for those accepting the principle that each
administrator can be valued as a member of a
total management team while agreeing that everyone has strengths and weaknesses.

MARYLAND'S "PROJECT BASIC"

Hornbeck, David W. Educational Leadership, Volume
    35, November 1977, pp. 98-101.

Hornbeck reports on the adoption of Project
Basic by the Maryland State Board of Education in
December 1976 with a projected completion date in
1982. Project Basic stems from the proposition
that schooling is that set of learning experiences
aimed at competencies that lead to an effective and
satisfying adulthood.

Hornbeck discusses the five areas the Maryland
Program identified as the most cirtical areas in
which minimal competencies should be identified.
They are 1) basic skills (reading, writing, and
the ability to calculate), 2) the world of work,
3) the world of leisure, 4) citizenship, and
5) survival skills. Within these areas the
Maryland Program defines a range of minimal
competencies and requires their achievement for
graduation. Grade-by-grade minimal competencies
have been adopted in reading while mathematics
competencies were to be adopted by the end of
1977.

Hornbeck describes the basic questions which
the State Department of Education hopes to answer
by 1982. In what manner is schooling done? Where
does schooling take place? Who delivers schooling?
When does schooling take place?

Hornbeck cites six principal responsibilities
of schooling which range from measurable skills to
abstract self concepts which have been made a part
of the Maryland Mission of Schooling. He projects
success for Maryland's Project Basic which

ultimately aims at helping all youngster
effective and satisfying adulthood.

RELIABLE RATING SHEETS: A KEY TO EFFECTIVE
    TEACHER EVALUATION

King, Richard A.   NASSP Bulletin, Volume 63,
    December 1978, pp. 21-26.

King presents findings of a survey made of
teacher evaluation instruments used by 32 school
districts in two counties of western New York
during the 1976-1977 school year.

He analyzed the rating sheets to determine
criteria that were most often rated during classroom observations and to determine which of those
indicators cited in the literature were included
in the rating sheets. King identified five
categories of criteria which are 1) personal
characteristics, 2) classroom management, 3)
relationships with community and staff 4) relationships with pupils, and 5) lesson planning and
presentation. Reports of the percentage of the
districts employing each criterion in rating
instruments and the number of times concepts
appeared to be measured in the instruments are
presented in tabular form. Concepts rated most
often were motivation and reinforcement, task
orientation, and warmth. Those rated least were
enthusiasm, indirectness, listening, probing
behavior, and questioning.

The author concludes that over 80% of the
rating instruments analyzed contained items to
assess such personal characteristics as voice,
speech, and use of English; management of the
physical conditions of the classroom; pupil
participation in lessons; control of the class
and rapport with students; lesson planning and
preparation, effective use of materials, methods,
and time, and adaptation of instruction to individual needs and capacities. King notes that many of
the criteria used in rating teacher performance

did not fall within categories identified in the
literature as related to teaching effectiveness.

Based upon the results of the investigation,
King makes two recommendations: 1) administrators
and teachers should cooperatively assess and
review rating sheets to increase the reliability
and effectiveness of classroom observation and
evaluation; and 2) two rating sheets should be
developed, one to be used in periodic classroom
observations to assess teaching performance and
the other designed to provide feedback on an
annual basis concerning performance of additional
responsibilities assumed by teachers.

MAINSTREAMING AS A NATURAL EXPERIENCE

Merz, Carol. Educational Leadership, Volume 37,
    February 1980, pp. 438-440.

The author reports upon a program that
developed in a small school with a high percentage
of handicapped children. The children and teachers
involved came together by accident when overcrowd-
ing forced some classes to move to a part of the
school separated from the main building. The
group included four first-grade classes and two
classes of multiply-handicapped children.

Merz states that during the first year no
planned interaction took place. However, informal
contacts were made as all students were obliged
to share the same facilities and the handicapped
and non-handicapped children became accustomed to
each other.

During the second year, one handicapped child
who seemed very bright was included in one of the
first-grade classes. Because the severity of the
handicaps prevented most of the other children
from participating in the regular curriculum,
Merz reports that teachers sent some first graders
into the special education classes to play with
the children,and some served as "coaches"

in preparing the handicapped children to participate in the Special Olympics.

One special education teacher and one first
grade teacher worked together to work out mainstreaming approaches. The author notes the increase
of self-reliance and ability to communicate on the
part of the handicapped children. She also reports
that the tolerance and understanding developed by
the non-handicapped children has increased and
maintains that friendships have been formed in a
wider circle than would have occurred otherwise.

Merz states that mainstreaming may just
possibly be a natural experience when teachers
look at each child as an individual and think of
ways to provide the best experience for each
child's development.

SPLIT-SCREEN VIDEOTAPING: THE GENIE IN THE BOTTLE

Moritz, William and Jo Anne Martin-Reynolds.
    Educational Leadership, Volume 37, February
    1980, pp. 396-399.

The authors report on the use of split-screen
videotaping with the teacher on one-half of the
screen and the students on the other as implemented
in Ohio as an alternative to traditional evaluation
in the improvement of instruction. The technique
was first used in the Maumee City Schools in 1971.
At present 157 Ohio districts have adopted the
process, and the Maumee district has 75% of the
instructional staff using the technique. Additionally, a variation of the process has been used in
preservice education at Bowling Green State
University, Bowling Green, Ohio, with the result
that subjects' attention was redirected away from
self toward teaching and student reaction.

Moritz and Martin-Reynolds state that research
conclusions and recommendations concerning video-
tape feedback have been generally favorable, even
in cases where no significant differences have

141

been found between playback and control groups. The authors' experience lead them to conclude that the critical component in modifying instructional behavior seems to be the feedback of teaching episodes that the teacher can accept as valid.

The authors recommend that nine hours of inservice training for teachers and administrators precede the first videotaping experience to provide understanding of the theory base and process of the model. During training, emphasis is placed on teacher acceptance of the responsibility for self-renewal and the development of an administrator/teacher team approach in the improvement of instruction. Prior to videotaping in the classroom, the teacher presents a microteaching lesson to peers and participates in a brief practice taping in the classroom. Following the actual classroom taping, the tape is given to the teacher to be reviewed first from a nonverbal viewpoint with the sound off and from a verbal aspect with the picture off. As a result of the self-analysis the teacher identifies one or two verbal and nonverbal criteria for improvement.

Based upon extensive field experience and feedback from teachers, the authors suggest three or four videotaped sessions the first year, 20 minutes in length spaced about a month apart, with lesser frequency in ensuing years, contingent upon individual differences and levels of acceptance of self and other human variables.

Moritz and Martin-Reynolds stress the positive aspects of the program, noting the advantage for the supervisor to schedule appointments with teachers to review the tapes before and after school when things are less hectic and the advantage to both parties in having a common frame of reference upon which to base a discussion and/or evaluation of the teacher's work.

S.C.A.P.E. FROM STIGMA: WILL YOUR MIDDLE SCHOOL
   BE READY FOR P.L. 94-142?

Morrill, Leslie T. Clearing House, Volume 52,
   May 1979, pp. 456-457.

   The author reports on the S.C.A.P.E. (Students
Care About Placement in Education) program as it
operates in Newark, Delaware to allow handicapped
children to "escape" labeling in classes and the
stigmatism associated with removal from the
regular classroom, with advantages to the students
and teachers. Six important administrative
decisions facilitate the program. They are 1) all
students are heterogeneously grouped; 2) the
teachers are arranged by teams; 3) each team
shares the same planning period; 4) each team is
assigned a resource teacher who shares the planning
periods of the teams of that grade and coordinates
the S.C.A.P.E. program; 5) the administration
emphasizes individualized consideration in instruction for all students; and 6) one period per day is
scheduled for student participation in band, chorus,
and other activities.

   The program provides a resource teacher who
works with the regular teacher in assessing
strengths and weaknesses in learning styles. The
person contacts parents of referred students to
obtain written permission for further evaluation.
Following the evaluation, the team of teachers,
the parent, and the resource teacher meet to
determine an appropriate plan for the student.
The process is repeated once a calendar year.

   Morrill notes that the key to the success of
S.C.A.P.E. is the constant communication between
the regular classroom teacher and the resource
teacher which is made possible by shared planning
time. The resource teacher works in the regular
classroom with both handicapped and non-handicapped
students to minimize possible stigmatism. The
constant communication between the teachers helps
the regular teacher to feel comfortable working
with the handicapped students.

143

MULTIPLE OPTION GRADE CONTRACTS

Partin, Ronald L. Clearing House, Volume 53,
    November 1979, pp. 133-135.

The author presents the multiple option grade
contract as a practical method of adapting a
criterion-referenced evaluation program to the
traditional and generally required letter grade.
Partin has used the method in a variety of high
school and college courses and recommends the
following contract: 100 points = A; 80 points =
B; 60 points = C. Partin notes that thus far no
one has requested a contract for a D.

Students are introduced to the contract at
the first class meeting. Each week from two to
ten activities keyed to course objectives are
assigned. Some activities reflecting vital skills
may be required of all students while other tasks
are optional, reflecting individual needs, values,
or interests. In order for the program to work
effectively, assignments need to be clearly stated
and deadlines need to be set for completion of
activities. Successful completion of each task
is accepted as mastery of a particular task.

Partin recommends that the total number of
points available should usually be at least double
the sum required for an A. The contract is
cumulative and positive. Students receive points
for achievement and effort.

The author lists 5 advantages recognized as
a result of implementation of this program:
1) the responsibility for grades is the student's
and the relationship between performance and grade
is apparent, 2) the flexible grade contract provides
an opportunity to individualize instruction and
assignments, 3) this method of grading encourages
the teacher to reflect upon the goals for the
course, 4) students compete with themselves not
their peers, and 5) the method is fair and the
subjective elements of out-psyching the teacher
are minimized.

MINIMUM COMPETENCIES -- THE OREGON APPROACH

Savage, David G. Educational Leadership, Volume
    36, October 1978, pp. 12-15.

    Sure, children go to school for 12 years, but
can they get along in the real world? This is the
question Savage deals with in his discussion of
Oregon's approach to miminum competencies. In
Oregon each school district established its own
set of competency standards and range of competencies.

    The Portland school district devised 12
standards while Beaverton public schools have
developed 127 competency standards. The variances,
among other things, have caused much confusion and
complaints. Some other problems encountered by
the school districts included an uncertainty as
to the definition of a minimum competency, the
paper work involved, the amount of time required,
and the question if passing of the test should
be required for graduation.

    District administrators and teachers requested
guidelines and models for use in developing competency standards from the State Department. They
also requested clarification on whether a student
should just acquire knowledge or demonstrate
knowledge on specific tasks.

    Oregon's Superintendent of Public Instruction
and the state board's definition of a competency
is that it should represent demonstrable ability
to apply knowledge, understanding, and/or skills.
The superintendent and the state board reviewed
the competency program in Oregon. Their findings
pointed out the need for the state department to
establish more uniform requirements among the
districts and to provide help for students in
need of remediation.

    Savage states that Oregon's program is a
sincere and thoughtful effort put forth by many
administrators and teachers. He reports that

curriculum directors in the school districts indicate that more good than bad has been brought about by the competency program. However, Savage comments that Oregon's approach has far to go in establishing its specific educational goals.

OTHER REFERENCES

Bailey, Gerald D. "Student Self-Assessment: Helping Students Help Themselves," Kappa Delta Pi Record, Volume 15, February 1979, pp. 86-88.

Browne, M. Neil, Paul F. Haas, and Stuart Keeley. "Measuring Critical Thinking Skills in College," The Educational Forum, Volume 42, January 1978, pp. 219-226.

Bryson, Seymour, Harold Bardo and Mary Ann Keiner. "Students' Perceptions and Evaluation of an Educational Opportunity Tutorial Program," College Student Journal, Volume 12, Summer 1978, pp. 135-139.

DeJulio, Ellen L. "Many Happy Returns," Today's Education, Volume 69, February-March 1980, pp. 72-73.

Farr, Roger and Bruce Tone. "What Does Research Show?" Today's Education, Volume 67, November-December 1978, pp. 33-36.

Hannon, Joseph P. and Michael Katims. "The Chicago Plan: Mastery Learning in the Chicago Public Schools," Educational Leadership, Volume 37, November 1979, pp. 120-122.

Lewis, Donald Marion. "Testing and Its Legal Limits - the Florida Decision," Today's Education, November-December 1979, pp. 25-28.

Munday, Leo A. "Changing Test Scores, Especially Since 1970," Phi Delta Kappan, Volume 60, March 1979, pp. 496-499.

Pipho, Chris. "Minimum Competency Testing in 1978: A Look at State Standards," Phi Delta Kappan, Volume 59, May 1978, pp. 585-587.

Rodriguez, Domingo A. "Bilingual Education: The Quest for Diversity and Quality," Educational Leadership, Volume 36, February 1979, pp. 341-343.

Sandberg, John H. "K-12 Competency-Based Education Comes to Pennsylvania," Phi Delta Kappan, Volume 61, October 1979, pp. 119-120.

Vukovich, Diane and Isobel Pfeiffer. "Self-Concept and Self-Evaluation: What is the Relationship?" Action in Teacher Education, Volume II, Winter, 1979-80, pp. 49-53.

Williams, Eugene. "Assessing Teacher Competencies with the Audiovisual Portfolio," Educational Leadership, Volume 37, December 1979, pp. 246-247.

Yarbourough, Betty H. and Roger A. Johnson. "Research That Questions the Traditional Elementary School Marking System," Phi Delta Kappan, Volume 61, April 1980, pp. 527-528.

Zettel, Jeffrey J. and Frederick J. Weintraub. "PL 94-142: Its Origins and Implications," National Elementary Principal, Volume 58, October 1978, pp. 10-13.

CHAPTER VII
STUDENT BEHAVIOR

Student behavior is influenced by cultural factors and shaped by many pressures involving both internal and external sources. The attitudes of administrators and teachers and the climate of individual schools determine student behavior to a great extent. A positive, humanistic school and classroom setting lays the foundation for affective learning to take place. Human relations are enhanced by administrators and teachers who empathize with students and who utilize a variety of appropriate strategies for coping such as behavior modification or the teaching of values. Moral education and the development of self-concept are also included in affective mental health programs which stress positive outcomes.

Although there are various programs relating to affective and humanistic education, student behavior remains a problem area in many classrooms across the country. Problems associated with student behavior include the relationship of nutrition to behavior, drug abuse, absenteeism, dropouts, suspension methods, children of divorce, and legal implications. Schools have developed and maintain various programs to facilitate and improve student behavior. Some common characteristics emerge from these programs with an emphasis on increasing each student's respect and concern for self and others, developing interpersonal skills for solving social problems, establishing group discussions where problems are explored, and understanding and accepting individual differences. Designers of these programs feel that learning to relate to others is as important as learning the three R's, and parental involvement is needed to assist in accomplishing the desired human relations outcome.

National research studies have revealed that between 15 and 30 percent of all students exhibit

149

emotional or behavioral problems at one time or another during the school year. Over 90 percent of these students are in regular, not special classrooms. Thus, it becomes apparent that teachers need some type of training to handle these student behavior problems. Assertive training is an example of one technique being utilized by many educators. The assertive approach to discipline and behavior is a systematic one which enables teachers to be firm and consistent while incorporating each student's need for positive support in the overall plan. The ultimate objective is reached when students learn to take responsibility for their own actions.

One starting point for improved student behavior has been recent studies revealing the close relationship between student behavior and nutrition. The nutritional habits and the somewhat strange diets of students have been directly or indirectly linked to hyperactive behavior, withdrawal symptoms, and lack of energy to complete classroom tasks. Teachers and physicians have an opportunity to combine forces in this critical area to seek education improvement through better nutrition. The relationship between drug abuse and student misbehavior has been generally accepted. This is a particularly tough problem for teachers, the medical profession, and legal juvenile authorities to solve. The victims are students who are not reached in time. Programs in drug abuse prevention have generally experienced many problems and few successes, but the work continues to assist students in this most difficult area.

The related problems of absenteeism, dropouts, and suspension methods have been around for a long time. Current programs place emphasis on positive outcomes developed in the individual classroom or school. For example, many suspension methods now include in-school suspension programs or an alternative classroom or school designed to give individual attention to the suspended student, the potential dropout, and the student who is absent too much. Group discussions, parental involvement,

150

and one-to-one counseling are utilized to a great
extent in these programs. Generally, they are
designed to make the individual aware of human
dignity and the supportive attitude of others.
Although children of divorce are in a different
category, these students also need warmth and
support from their teachers and administrators
as they cope with this most difficult period in
their lives.

Most student behavior problems have legal
implications for administrators, teachers and
parents, and students. Teachers and administrators
must be cognizant of court rulings affecting student
dress, student disruption, student suspension, and
student due process as guaranteed by the First
Amendment. Before an educator can be supportive,
it may be necessary to check the existing laws,
rules, and regulations pertaining to student
misbehavior/discipline problems.

A coordinated student advisement program
involving administrators, counselors, and teachers
is being used by some schools to assist students
with behavioral problems by providing opportunities
for student self-control, self-direction, and
individually tailored educational experiences.
This type advisement program facilitates continuous
assessment and analysis of existing curriculum.
It entails determining the extent to which students'
needs are being met, identification of student
problems, selection of appropriate means for solving problems, and evaluation of progress toward
meeting students' needs and problems. The administrator sets the pace, opens doors, and makes
resources available. Accordingly, instructional
personnel are freed from administrative trivia
enabling them to spend full time in implementation
of curriculum according to individual student needs.

It is obvious that educators need certain
skills to work successfully in the area of student
behavior. In addition to the affective, supportive
skills needed to work with these problems, educators need training in legal matters, nutritional

studies, drug abuse techniques, and individual/ group counseling techniques. Forces influencing student behavior include legal decisions, federal and state programs, more student freedom, changing family lifestyles, and the overall cultural environment. Positive student behavior is best developed and maintained in a supportive but firm and consistent climate of caring. To accomplish this outcome is one of the more formidable challenges which concerned educators have to cope with at the present time.

Educational leaders are placing increasing emphasis on relevance and motivation in the curriculum. This position recognizes that students have a need to know that they are capable of achieving personal and vocational skills for future fulfillment and employment. Recognizing this need of students, educators are implementing supportive, relevant personalized programs which develop positive student behavior. Such programs accompanied by effective teaching are providing means for improving student behavior.

SYNOPSES

DISCIPLINE: IF YOU DO THAT AGAIN, _____

Barth, Roland S. Phi Delta Kappan, Volume 61,
    February 1980, pp. 398-400.

Barth describes the Angier School in Newton,
Massachusetts, which has developed an elaborate
disciplinary process characterized by concern,
consistency, and consequences. Enforcement of
rules is a major school problem. If students
know that something will happen if they misbehave,
this can become a powerful force for changing
behavior. At the elementary level, discipline
is a less serious problem than it is at the
secondary level. But it is still a problem due
to the way limited repertoire of responses to
misbehavior and the unpredictability with which
these meager responses are employed.

At Angier School, the faculty developed
three parallel sets of student rules and three
different kinds of consequences when they were
violated. The first set deals with each teacher's
individual classes where each teacher establishes
rules for students in that class. Children are
not sent to the principal's office for breaking
classroom rules; rather, teachers assume responsibility for their own classroom rules. These
rules vary from teacher to teacher. The second
set of rules are formally stated expectations for
children which govern behavior in common areas
such as halls, assemblies, and playgrounds. In
these situations, diversity is neither workable
nor acceptable;therefore, only a few uniform
policies are determined and enforced through
teacher involvement. The third set of rules is
for children who repeatedly violate either
classroom rules or the rules of common areas. In
these situations the principal, the school
psychologist, and the parents must become involved
to support the teacher and to provide the child
with more and different kinds of adult control.

Working with these children involves referrals to specialists, conferences with key supportive personnel, specific guidelines to the student and parents, and possible one day suspensions at home.

Barth concludes that learning to live within the constraints of the school society is as important a preparation for life in a larger society as is knowledge of the multiplication tables. Clear expectations and specific consequences for misbehavior have lessened this school's problems since it initiated the three level system.

POSITIVE DISCIPLINE: A PRACTICAL APPROACH TO DISRUPTIVE STUDENT BEHAVIOR

Bourgeois, Don. NASSP Bulletin, Volume 63, September 1979, pp. 68-71.

Bourgeois describes a program at Carenco High School in Lafayette, Louisiana, which was designed to provide a preventive approach to the handling of student disruptions. The program consists of two parts: 1) an inservice program based on Berne's Transactional Analysis designed to help teachers understand better what is happening in transactions between two people, and 2) a psychological model based on Glasser's Reality Theory that attempts to change student behavior. The author states that there must be a balance between psychology and sound administrative practices in the area of discipline.

The Glasser Reality Therapy model helps teachers see that many times they are the cause of student behavior, yet the student must be made to realize that he has the total responsibility of his own behavior. The program also stresses that the student must suffer the consequences of his/her own behavior, since the consequences have been explained in advance. A student goes through certain steps after the disruptive classroom behavior. These steps begin with a one-to-one

154

conference with the classroom teacher, a conference with a grade level counselor, communication to parents, and a one-to-one conference with the self-discipline teacher. For the first three suspensions, students go to a Self-Discipline Center, a room within the school staffed with a special teacher. The fourth suspension brings expulsion and a hearing in the central office with the student readmitted on probation to the Self-Discipline Center. The fifth suspension brings expulsion from school.

Bourgeois states that teachers were concerned about how to handle the one-to-one conference with students. They were given four steps to follow: 1) let the student know you care about his problem, 2) have the student recall the behavior which initiated the trouble, 3) develop options with consequences for unacceptable behavior, and 4) finally, get a written commitment or contract from the student about the individual's behavior. The author concludes that the program is beneficial because it provides a teacher and a place, the Self Discipline Center, where students returning from suspension can be helped to find alternatives to their unacceptable behavior.

PRINCIPALS' ATTITUDES ON STUDENT ABSENTEEISM: A SURVEY REPORT

Brimm, Jack L., John Forgety, and Kenneth Sadler. NASSP Bulletin, Volume 62, February 1978, pp. 65-69.

Brimm, Forgety, and Sadler surveyed Tennessee high school principals concerning their attitudes toward problems of student absenteeism. Eighty-three percent returned completed questionnaires. Eighty-six percent of the principals reported student absenteeism as a major problem, but only 50 percent indicated that their absentee rate had increased. Most principals felt that discipline, not student absenteeism, was their foremost problem, and 40 indicated that schools do not place enough emphasis on regular attendance. The principals identified compulsory attendance laws, change in students' attitudes toward authority and school, and erosion of parental control as the primary forces leading to increased absenteeism. They felt that existing laws contributed to the absenteeism problem by confining the unwilling learner and agreed that there is a group of students that resist any method of compulsory attendance.

The principals indicated that male students stay out more than female students, and that juniors and seniors stay out more than younger classmates. The lower the grades and less popular the student the higher the absentee rate. Absenteeism is a greater problem on Monday and Friday and during the second semester. The principals listed the following suggestions to alleviate the problem: 1) reorganization of Monday and Friday activities, 2) use of simulation exercises, 3) curriculum modification, 4) student surveys, and 5) workshops to focus on daily classroom routine and causes of absenteeism.

BEHAVIOR MODIFICATION IN AN ELEMENTARY SCHOOL: PROBLEMS AND ISSUES

Elardo, Richard. Phi Delta Kappan, Volume 59, January 1978, pp. 334-338.

Elardo reports on an experiment in behavior modification conducted by the Center for Child Development and Education at Kramer School in Little Rock, Arkansas. A large grant from the federal Office of Child Development made possible a five-year project to improve and humanize all aspects of this inner-city school. The goal was to produce a working model of a comprehensive child development facility and school. One of the main efforts of the program was to provide teachers with an alternative to corporal punishment. Kramer is a small elementary school of 175 students with grades one through five. The school has seven classrooms with a 60:40 black/white ratio.

The school had many nagging discipline problems including fighting, abuse of school property and disrespect for teachers. Certain teachers in the school relied on corporal punishment maintaining that this was the type of punishment children received at home. Other teachers questioned this approach and were searching for an alternative method of improving behavior. A school-wide plan of behavior modification was chosen as a means of improving behavior. Much time was spent by teachers in discussing and understanding the plan before it went into effect. The plan called for token rewards for good behavior throughout the school. Tokens could be traded in once a week on Thursday or Friday afternoon for rewards. These rewards varied from beauty parlor treatments to parties, tennis lessons, sewing lessons, rocket launching, or a trip to the airport. Each activity had a price and students had to earn enough tokens to buy the things they wanted. The students who did not have enough tokens to buy anything were sent to a "helping room" where they were assigned work under the supervision of a staff member.

After six weeks most teachers were enthusiastic, but the recommendation was made that all bank balances would return to zero at the end of each week so that students would not build up big balances and then misbehave. The fifth graders complained about this new rule,and the staff viewed this protest favorably since it showed initiative and concern on the part of the students. A compromise agreeable to students was worked out.

In January students were polled as to what price should be charged for each reward activity, and the results of the poll were used for price-fixing. Also plastic chips for rewards were found unsatisfactory,and a system of checks by students' names was posted at the end of each day.

157

Problems perceived by the author were that
some teachers were less enthusiastic and some
children never got enough tokens to buy a reward
activity. These students who earned no rewards
were still a discipline problem when they were
sent to the helping room. While this approach
to better behavior may be difficult to put into
effect, it provides students a realistic opportunity to learn how the democratic system works
with its checks and balances.

TWENTY-FIVE NINE YEAR-OLDS MAKE A FILM

Freeman, Jayne. Phi Delta Kappan, Volume 61,
     November 1979, pp. 173, 188, 226-227.

     Freeman describes her fourth grade students'
involvement with film-making at the Seth Lewelling
School in Milwaukie, Oregon. The fourth graders
planned and performed all phases of the film-
making project. Student interest, behavior, and
involvement were crucial factors in this project.
As time progressed, the students developed the
plot, operated the cameras, added the sound track,
and edited the film all under the supervision of
a professional film-maker who was experienced in
working with young children.

     The students spent the first few days
deciding upon a title and details of the plot
for their film. The film was "Cattlestar
Galactica." The spaceship would transport
cattle to the planets that needed milk. The
bad guys were called the "butcheroids " and stole
the cattle. The Butcheroids and Cattlestars would
then have an old-fashioned shoot out. After the
plot details were worked out, the students worked
on scenery and sound effects. The back wall was
used as background for space shots. Every week
the students previewed and edited the previous
week's film. They observed flaws and improved
the filming. After editing the film, the students
developed a sound script and added it to the film.

158

Even the disruptive students were quiet when the need arose.

The students enjoyed a sense of pride and accomplishment with the finished product, and the film was entered in the District Art Fair and the Northwest Film Study Center's Annual Children's film festival. The Center wrote a good commentary about the film, saying it was the best of the year. Additionally, the film was shown on television so the public could view it. This project demonstrated that young children can stay with a long-term project with consistency. The students in the project demonstrated a sense of group cohesiveness, while experiencing growth in art skills, attention span, independence, and self-control.

AN APPROACH TO STUDENT MISBEHAVIOR

Fuchs, Julius E., James D. Fenn, and John T. Reid. NASSP Bulletin, Volume 62, January 1978, pp. 98-103.

Fuchs, Fenn, and Reid describe a Behavioral Attitude Change Program at North Junior High School in Pittsfield, Massachusetts as an approach to changing student misbehavior and attitude. The program has been implemented as a small group counseling program designed for students with behavior disorders and is used in lieu of continuing punishment. Some of the behaviors dealt with are truancy, lack of motivation, classroom disruption, cutting class, lack of self-control, and homelife problems that cause misbehavior.

A counseling group is composed of approximately eight boys and girls with a counselor which meets for forty-five minutes. The program has three phases. First is the introduction where the goals and objectives are explained. Also, in this phase, it is stressed that each student needs to voice an opinion as to what is important to him/her and discuss why he/she is there. The second phase is the group discussion when some ground rules are established. Discussions are

159

free and open, and confidentiality is evident.
During this phase, the greatest amount of flexibility needs to be used. Misbehavior is a many-
sided problem and one approach does not correct
all situations. If Transactional Analysis is
used and does not produce change, then another
method needs to be incorporated. One of the most
difficult problems here is trying to combat low
self-esteem, but hopefully one successful approach
will help restore feelings of worthiness and
feelings of being appreciated. This phase is of
great importance because it is here that students
can talk with someone they can trust, feel
comfortable with, and have a relaxed, non-
threatening climate. The last phase is that of
a follow-up where contact is made with each student
who has left the group.

The authors caution that after leaving the
program, possible behavior regression may occur;
therefore continuous student contact with
administrators and teachers is very important.
This contact serves as a reminder of the student's
responsibilities and provides moral support.
Through follow-up, it has been noted that one in
three students have made a significant change in
behavior while others show varying degrees of
change.

THE STRIDE PROGRAM: AN ANSWER TO ABSENTEEISM

Hakanen, Lauri John. Phi Delta Kappan, Volume 59,
    January 1978, pp. 348-349.

    Hakanen discusses the Students and Teachers
Really Interested in Dropout Education (STRIDE)
Program developed in 1976 in the Harlem School
District of Rockford, Illinois. The program was
designed to enable students to gain academic
success and reduce potential dropouts in the
district.

    Hakanen describes the STRIDE Program as an
alternative in which students deal with only one

160

teacher in a self-contained situation while
studying the basic subjects of English, computation skills, science, and social studies during
an abbreviated three-hour school day. They also
study problems of getting and holding a job
during this half-day in school. During the other
half of the day,they seek employment or work
outside the school with a high percentage being
employed.

Benefits of the program include improved
staff morale, increased community support, and
increased interest in school with an improved
self-concept on the part of the student. The
staff accepts the program and recommends it for
certain students. More students are seeking
admission to the program than can be accommodated.

Hanaken's conclusion is that the STRIDE
Program can be a viable alternative to the regular
school if three requirements are accomplished:
1) quality multi-discipline teachers involved
in the program, 2) a reduction in fear of the
change process in the local school district, and,
3) the support of the total school staff. Without the supportive efforts of administrators
and teachers, programs such as this cannot be
effective. Involvement in the program has
assisted in developing more positive student
behavior.

DRUG ABUSE AND YOUR CHILD: WHAT CAN THE SCHOOLS
    DO?

Kearney, Artie L. The School Counselor, Volume
    26, January 1979, pp. 187-190.

Kearney reports on the Drug Prevention
Education program developed by Cooperative
Educational Service Agency Number Eight (CESA #8)
in Appleton, Wisconsin. This program is unique
because it focuses on the reasons why children
abuse drugs rather than on the drugs themselves.

The CESA #8 Drug Prevention Education Program is for children in grades two through six. However, many of the activities can be developed for kindergarten and first grade. The major goals of this program are to help students feel better about themselves, to provide students with problem-solving skills, and to stimulate healthy attitudes toward the application and misapplication of drugs. The training for this program includes a general overview of the program and videotape demonstrations of students and teachers doing some of the program activities. These activities are presented in teacher and/or student activity packages. The packages contain value clarification exercises, exercises focusing on the development of self, decision-making exercises, and exercises pertaining to information about drugs relevant to students' lives.

The CESA #8 project staff conducted an evaluative study to measure the program's effectiveness in primary and intermediate level students. Pretests and posttests were administered to experimental schools with the program and control groups without the program. Based on the result of this evaluative study, the CESA #8 Drug Prevention Education Program significantly improved the students' feelings of self-worth, significantly increased students' decision-making abilities, increased students' factual knowledge about drugs, and improved the students' attitudes toward the use and misuse of drugs.

According to Kearney, presently this program is believed to be the only known exemplary elementary level drug prevention program being disseminated throughout the country. This program reaches the children before they start drug abuse.

HOW SCHOOLS CAN HELP THE CHILDREN OF DIVORCE

Kelly, Joan B. and Judith S. Wallerstein. The
    National Elementary Principal, Volume 59,
    October 1979, pp. 51-58.

Kelly and Wallerstein report on part of a five
year longitudinal study by the Children of Divorce
Project in Greenbrae, California, involving 60
northern California divorcing families and their
131 children, ages 3 to 18 at the time of marital
separation. With few exceptions, the children in
the study viewed their parents' separation and
divorce as extremely stressful. Since the school
is the most continuous institution in the lives of
the many children whose parents divorce, the authors
sought to determine to what extent children in
crisis can use the school as a supportive network.

Kelly and Wallerstein found first that school
was useful in providing structure in a child's life
at a time when the major structure of life, the
family, was crumbling. Second, there was the
support provided to those children who enjoyed
coming to school and whose particular academic
achievements sustained and nourished them. Third,
some children were helped by their close relationship with, and reliance on, a friendly teacher.
In general, however, the authors found that fewer
children really used or were capable of falling
back on the school network than they had expected
to find. They also found little evidence to suggest
that the availability of the school as a support
system shared the child's eventual outcomes.

Kelly and Wallerstein suggest that schools in
the future become more involved with the children
of divorce. The authors list some ways in which
schools can provide additional help for these
children: 1) teacher awareness of divorce and the
associated problems, 2) teacher willingness to help,
3) after-school care by the school for children up
to 12, and 4) adult education programs on divorce.
Kelly and Wallerstein conclude by noting that it is

critical for teachers and principals to be sensitive
to the ways in which the stress of family breakup
can disrupt their students' ability to participate
in the learning process.

MEET CHARLES HEAD

Needham, Nancy. Today's Education, Volume 68,
    September-October 1979, pp. 54-58.

Needham interviews and describes the methods
utilized by Charles Head, a chemistry teacher at
Hillcrest High School in Dallas, Texas. Six years
ago, he set up an activity the students call DC,
which stands for Discipline Committee. This group
has functioned as a device for serving a distinct
portion of the Hillcrest student population, the
angry, the disaffected, and the ones who are close
to dropping out. The Discipline Committee was
formed as a result of a federal court order which
mandated the first major cross-town busing in
Dallas. White students from the bottom of the
socioeconomic ladder clashed with a group of
black students who were bused in to see which
group could push the other down. One of the first
actions was to call in the 12 to 15 leaders of
the problem to talk with assistant principals and
teachers.

Since the beginning, the Discipline Committee
has continued to work on individual problems. Each
individual gets to talk in front of a group of
fellow students. The Discipline Committee also
brings in the parents because mental health is
the number one health problem in the country and
parents must play a role in supporting students
with problems. In addition to the Discipline
Committee, Head used his science classes to help
low-ability students with problems. He did this
through a special course called Man-Made World,
a nonmathematical science course taught with a
colleague. The course was very successful, but
the school system overloaded the two teachers with
too many problem students, increasing the class load

from 15-20 to 30-32. Finally, the course was dropped, but the Discipline Committee continues to function in helping problem students to solve their own problems at Hillcrest High School.

DIET AND SCHOOL CHILDREN

Phlegar, Fred L. and Barbara Phlegar. Phi Delta Kappan, Volume 61, September 1979, pp. 53-56.

Phlegar and Phlegar review several situations around the country relating to nutrition and make the assumption that like medical doctors, educators have been slow to realize how often there is a direct relationship between the kinds of food children consume today and their behavior and academic achievement. The authors discuss ten cases from different sections of the United States which describe specific instances in which a relationship between food and behavior is suspected. Foods cited as troublemakers include sugar, milk, eggs, corn, wheat, citrus products, beef, pork, caffeine, and additives. A typical case study usually involves a hyperactive youngster who constantly moves, squirms, drums his fingers, and generally annoys other students. After a diet adjustment, the youngster usually calms down, has an increased attention span, and achieves more academically.

Phlegar and Phlegar note several problems which may make it difficult for all school systems to do much about the foods they serve and about student eating habits. First, multi-billion-dollar food packing companies do not want America's student eating habits changed just as the tobacco industry does not want America's smoking habits changed. There are also huge profits in junk food products for the schools themselves. Parents are often not at home to monitor students' eating habits. Another problem is that many individuals do not believe that the products which contain sugar, caffeine, additives, salt, and certain other foods can be harmful. Finally, the medical

165

profession itself does not generally support the primary thesis that behavior can be changed by diet. It appears that there is a great need for more study, research, and dissemination in nutrition education.

A MODEST STRATEGY FOR REDUCING SCHOOL CONFLICT

Reed, Rodney J. and Joan P. Avis. NASSP Bulletin, Volume 63, February 1979, pp. 26-38.

Reed and Avis describe a student-centered preventive model for reducing school conflict, its implementation in a Northern California School District, and the participants' reactions to it. This project focused on student advocacy as a method of dealing with conflict by means of the Conflicts Management Student Leadership Program.

The major objectives of the project were 1) to assist students in identifying conflicts and tensions in the schools and to develop skills in their resolution; 2) to facilitate student personal growth and development; 3) to assist students in developing more effective interpersonal relationships with students, school staff, community, and parents; and 4) to assist students in understanding school policy, governance, and the dimensions of students' rights.

According to the authors, three groups of 25 students from each of three senior high schools were chosen for leadership potential, reflecting a numerical balance on the basis of ethnicity, sex, and grade level. A final selection criterion for approximately one-half of the students was involvement in some school-related conflict that resulted in disciplinary action. Effort was made to create a heterogeneous group of students that reflected the mix one would find in a typical urban school. These persons engaged in a training program planned for 72 student contact hours. Students in the program received compensation for each hour of

166

participation, were provided lunch when training lasted the entire day, and were provided transportation from their schools to the training site.

Facilitators and training staff were selected for their professional training and expertise, work with adolescents, and their energy or enthusiasm. A variety of teaching techniques and media were used placing emphasis on developing a total community with a problem-solving atmosphere.

Participating students identified and explored actual and potential conflict and tension areas such as personal feelings, life-style patterns, sex stereotyping, communication, teaching styles, and community attitudes. They were encouraged to explore their family and peer relationships and to examine the basis for their negative and positive self-evaluation. They engaged in a variety of means to develop communication and group interaction skills. Particular attention was placed on understanding the school system; student motivation and incentives for school, family, and administrators; and the improvement of relations with each of them.

Reed and Avis concluded that the changes reported in the behavior of students are valid testimony to the success of CMSL, even though objective data is limited and procedural recommendations for other situations are difficult to translate. They surmise that the experience of participation in the project influenced student personal development.

INTER-SCHOOL PASSAGES: A PROGRAM FOR TRANSITION

Warchol, Kenneth J. The Clearing House, Volume 52, January 1979, pp. 233-235.

Warchol describes a humanistic orientation program for high school students in Norwalk, Connecticut, a city located in the New York metropolitan area with widely divergent racial, ethnic, and socio-economic groups. In order to ease opening day problems and humanize the first crucial days of a new school experience, the Assistant Superintendent for Human Relations established a task force to deal with this situation. The group was composed of faculty and administrators from three schools in the city - a secondary school, a middle school, and an elementary school.

As a first step for a smoother transition, students in each of the selected feeder schools held special sessions to brainstorm their antic- ipated concerns. There was a need for the task force to improve communications between schools and public relations in general based on the stu- ents' input. Various meetings were held for the students, and later in the spring, all parents and students met with the administrators and counselors of the school the students would be attending in the fall. Also, teachers of the grades bridging the three schools met informally to discuss individual situations. An element of peer coun- seling developed as former students returned to schools they had previously attended. For the September opening of school, the task force recommended and implemented a staggered opening, where each class new to a school had the facility, faculty, and staff to itself on the opening day. At the high school, many new orientation techniques were implemented.

Warchol notes that a major advantage of the concept of structured transition over many other educational programs is the fact that costs are minimal, although significant time is spent restructuring activities to make the orientation process more personal and humanistic. The program at Norwalk has incorporated many sound human rela- tions techniques to facilitate the transitions from elementary school to middle school to secondary school in a more humanistic manner.

STUDENTS CAN BE EFFECTIVE CHANGE AGENTS

Wright, Johnny. NASSP Bulletin, Volume 63,
    February 1979, pp. 44-49.

Wright describes a student participatory model
developed and implemented in the Pike County High
School at Brundidge, Alabama. The model was
designed specifically to eliminate drug abuse in
the school using student participation and peer
pressure to effect the desired change.

The essential factor in this model was based
on student involvement. According to certain
authorities on conflict and crisis management,
students are in a much better position than principals and teachers to transform schools into
desirable ways. A plan was developed which enabled
the students, faculty, and administration to plan
numerous activities as a team. Prom planning,
policy review and revision, intramural planning,
curriculum and senior day decisions were decided
through consensus where each member of the committee had equal rank and power. Students became
involved with decision-making procedures and were
part of the power structure of the school. This
open communication and interaction among the three
groups ensured an atmosphere conducive to con-
structive change.

Various programs were developed to facilitate
immediate and long-range change in the school drug
culture. A subcommittee formed a "rap-room" for
students to talk over problems on a one-to-one
basis with their peers. Another subcommittee
disseminated information to the student body about
alternatives to drug abuse and use. One very
important subcommittee contacted known drug users
on campus to persuade them to leave their drugs at
home. Peer pressure was applied on a one-to-one
encounter. Wright concludes that the application
of the appropriate peer pressure effectively
eliminated the drug abuse problem at Pike County
High School.

OTHER REFERENCES

Beck, Harriet C. "Teaching to Captivated Students: Juveniles in Custody," Journal of Reading, Volume 21, December 1977, pp. 235-239.

Burton, John K., Thomas C. Hunt, and Terry M. Wildman. "Who Transmits Values? The Public Schools," Educational Leadership, Volume 37, January 1980, pp. 314-318.

Calhoun, George Jr., and Raymond N. Elliott, Jr. "Self Concept and Academic Achievement of Educable Retarded and Emotionally Disturbed Pupils," Exceptional Children, Volume 43, March 1977, pp. 379-380.

Callard, Esther D. "Developing Socially Valued Behavior in Young Children," Childhood Education, Volume 4, November-December 1978, pp. 68-75.

Canter, Lee. "Taking Charge of Student Behavior," The National Elementary Principal, Volume 58, June 1979, pp. 33-36, 41.

Delattre, Edwin J. "Moral Education: A Response to Burton, Hunt, and Wildman," Educational Leadership, Volume 37, January 1980, pp. 319-320.

Dunlop, John. "Negotiating Student Discipline Policy," Today's Education, Volume 68, April-May 1979, pp. 27-30.

Elardo, Phyllis and Mark Cooper. "Project Aware: A Developmental Approach to Humanistic Education," Elementary School Guidance and Counseling, Volume 13, December 1978, pp. 112-122.

Harvey, Donald L. and William G. Moosha. "A Positive Alternate-In-School Suspension: Does It Work?" NASSP Bulletin, Volume 61, January 1977, pp. 14-17.

Hinkley, Ed. "An Instructional Program for Drop-outs," NASSP Bulletin, Volume 63, February 1979, pp. 59-64.

Horacek, Thelma. "The Discipline Dilemma," Today's Education, Volume 68, April-May 1979, pp. 20-21.

Hull, Howard. "In Defense of 'Frills'," Tennessee Education, Volume 8, Winter 1979, pp. 19-23.

Kobak, Dorothy. "Teaching Children to Care," Children Today, Volume 8, March-April 1979, pp. 6-7, 34-35.

Loviglio, Lorraine. "How Body Language Communicates in the Classroom," The Massachusetts Teacher, Volume 59, November 1979, pp. 6-14.

Mallory, Richard M. "The Teacher Who Disciplines Least," Today's Education, Volume 68, April-May 1979, pp. 23-26.

Martin, Barbara A. "The Slammer: An In-School Suspension Program," The Massachusetts Teacher, Volume 59, October 1979, pp. 91-97.

Nienstad, Serena. "Discipline for Today's Children," Phi Delta Kappan, Volume 60, April 1979, pp. 575-576.

Raymond, Edward. "A Volunteer Dropout Prevention Program," NASSP Bulletin, Volume 62, January 1978, pp. 91-97.

Strike, Kenneth A. and Robert C. Serow. "How Tolerant Are High School Students?," The Educational Forum, Volume XLII, March 1978, pp. 327-336.

Van Hoose, John. "The Effective Aide for Affective Education," Phi Delta Kappan, Volume 59, June 1978, pp. 674-675.

Woods, Harlan. "New Help for Troubled Youth," <u>Texas</u> <u>Outlook</u>, Volume 61, June 1977, pp. 19-22.

CHAPTER VIII
CURRICULUM PROCESSES AND PATTERNS

The effectiveness of public school education is being sorely questioned. Expectations of the products of the public schools from the general public and even educators are high and perhaps unrealistic. The once cherished idea that schools have all the answers to success is fast becoming passe. Numerous groups and individuals have taken steps to provide their own avenues of education. While the established systems of education have sought new and improved buildings, facilities, and technology, many other groups have set up schools in abandoned school buildings and private structures.

Surely this has a message for the traditional establishment. Shall we say the curriculum is the essence of the public's concern? The swing toward providing the ultimate in facilities and technology in some schools has seriously modified the curriculum - the content and experiences encountered by the learners. Open space buildings with all their educational possibilities have not necessarily brought about open education - a medium for providing curriculum experiences appropriate to the individual. Studies made to determine the effectiveness of open space buildings along with open education and of each separately have generally shown limited increase by students in the academic subject areas and considerable gain in self-concept and social virtues. This modification of facilities continues to broaden on one hand and be challenged on the other.

Educators are caught in a crossfire. The open conflicts of the sixties with students and schools have subsided. However, the attitude and tone of parents, teachers, and the general public, supported by legislation, court actions and pressure groups, are causing a more cautious approach to curriculum patterns, processes, and content. The Civil Rights movement of the 1960's, the counter-culture bilingual

173

programs, the British progressive schools, Philadelphia's experiences with schools without walls, Houston's magnet schools, to name a few, convinced many that schools do not have to be traditional to be effective. This has not sufficed for many, particularly in the face of the declining scores on national achievement tests. The back to the basics movement, Proposition 13, and other such pressures are having an impact on school curriculum and program offerings.

Historically the church was the early author of the educational processes. The Bible was the chief source of educational content and continued until recent years to provide the basis for significant educational experiences even in the public schools. Desegregation mandates have strengthened the well established parochial schools and nurtured countless new church schools under protestant church authorities. In spite of the separation of church and state doctrine of our constitution, federal funds have been provided to private and parochial schools that have affected curriculum processes.

One of the most significant movements affecting modification of curriculum content in public education has been the effort toward year round school programs. Even though the number of schools actually operating on a year round basis is insignificant, the development of curriculum content for dissemination in a quarter system has generated extensive study, rethinking, and re-organization of school curriculum content and experiences syllibi. This has brought about the offering of many new short courses not otherwise available to students and the breaking up of year long required courses in segments more feasible to students. By this means, students' programs and study emphases can be redirected at three month intervals rather than the annual pass or fail repeat a whole year course traditional procedure. Year round schooling creates an awareness of the need for fiscal responsibility and a change on

174

the labor force load factor in business. It eliminates the stop-and-go imbalances the traditional plan promulgates and utilizes resources, buildings, and personnel more efficiently. Nevertheless, in spite of the expressed value of the quarter system, many schools are now reorganizing the curriculum for longer blocks of study under the well known semester pattern.

Uninvolved students are being returned to education through the offerings and modified curriculum provided by drop-out centers, learning centers, and centers for the disruptive. Curriculums which provide for career education and instruction in technological developments are being engendered by societal emphases, job needs, and interests of youth. Some educators recommend that compulsory school attendance be lowered and that more attention be given to community centers which enable youth to gain job skill and learn the skills and rudiments of living in our complex society. This suggests that students be taught marketable skills and how to sell these skills to prospective employers. It assumes that by opening one door wide participating students will want to move on to other doors. It frees the bored and the frustrated from being locked into structured education not compatible to their disposition at the time. Many students unable to function in structured schools are functioning well in unstructured settings of open education. Here attention is given to learning where the action is - in the mill, retail stores, laboratory, library, city hall, or courtroom.

Curriculum processes and patterns are dangerously vulnerable to pressure groups and society's ups and downs. Recognizing that the basic responsibility for education was left to the states in our national constitution, many are concerned with the increasing impact the federal government is having on school curriculum. For example, curriculum equity in physical education for women and in language development for multi-ethnic and

175

bilingual persons has been federally mandated, thereby modifying and expanding the curriculum offerings in both areas. Federal support for career education and education for the handicapped has brought new emphases in content, new course offerings, and stringent modification of instructional procedures.

Probably the greatest threat to school curriculum is the lack of any systematic pattern for priortizing curriculum needs at state and local levels. Consequently it has been found that curriculum designs from school to school have little consistency. The failure of educators to pursue any agreed upon set of purposes and objectives in education has left schools open to attack by pressure groups with their favored brands of education. The specificity required in making application for federal programs has caused educators to become more adept in this needed area of writing and implementing programs according to well defined objectives.

The advent of federally funded research and development centers begun in the sixties produced a tremendous bank of curriculum materials and procedures. The current efforts of the National Institute of Education to evaluate and validate the more effective educational programs could provide a common body of data on which to establish some common objectives. It at least offers some patterns for curriculum development and modification for consideration by state and local curriculum developers.

The federal government's increased involvement in education during the last two decades has no doubt influenced the shift from the content oriented approach to a more practical approach to curriculum and instruction. This swing toward the practical, along with the changing attitude of youth toward education and many other factors, has brought about a strong call on the part of the general public for a "back to the basics" movement.

176

Some school systems have instituted plans whereby student progression in school is based almost totally on standard test scores.

Suffice to say there are situations which give attention to such processes as values clarification, travel for credit, utilization of human resources, and action phases involving independent study and problem solving. Numerous special features within school curriculum are reportedly being designed to respond to human needs and counteract the mechanical, factory thrust being felt in so many situations. Use of learning centers for student involvement with specific content is a well recognized effort in this direction.

The increasing emphasis on involving more persons and groups in curriculum decision making processes often overshadows the selection of content and experiences to be encountered by the learners. State legislatures are mandating that certain areas be included in the curriculum such as requiring all educators to have a course in special education. Accountability legislation ranges from mandated reporting to citizens by schools to state-wide standard high school exit examinations and certification of teachers, supervisors, and administrators, based on competency tests. Organized pressure groups attack directly textbook selections, course offerings, and programs which seem to reflect value positions. Too often views of such groups become the conscience of textbook publishers, legislators, and school administrators. Thereby curriculum decision making reflects the voices of the noisy minority and deprives individual learners and the masses of educators reasonable opportunity for participation.

Philosophy and goals of education have been modified considerably through federal acts such as PL 94-142. The education of all handicapped children act is based on the philosophy that supports individualized instruction, zero reject

177

admission, due process procedure, parent involvement, and mandatory integration thereby necessitating curriculum adapted to individual needs. Adoption of these tenets for the handicapped signals the acceptance of the philosophy of individualized education for all youth. Record keeping for individual education prescriptions (IEP) and the mechanics of due process are tantalizing. However, mastery of these technicalities through the aid of support personnel and other means may open the doors for more meaningful education long sought by many educators.

As is often the case trends run in counter acting pairs causing much consternation among curriculum developers. The very factors mandated in the education of all handicapped children act may be negated in the competency based legislation now so popular in the state capitols. Educational promotion based on minimum standards as determined by restricted testing may well deter implementation of the philosophy that every human being has a right to an education and to be treated as a human being. A grave concern is that the competency movement toward adequacy and literacy may mitigate toward the academically adequate and literate student who needs to go beyond the limited concept of education.

SYNOPSES

COOPERATIVE DEVELOPMENT OF PLANNING AND EVALUATION
SKILLS

Benjamin, Paula W. Educational Leadership,
    Volume 35, February 1978, pp. 401-403.

Benjamin describes the methods by which she
helped educators write plans for developing and
improving curriculum in 25 Los Angeles schools.
The plans, which included goals and objectives as
well as detailed explanations of how the goals
and objectives were to be reached, were submitted
to the California State Department of Education
in order for the schools to qualify for the
implementation of Early Childhood Education and
Title I Programs. To assist the writers of the
plans, Benjamin conducted three series of meetings
with administrators, project coordinators, and
selected teachers. Each series of meetings was
followed by similar meetings in the individual
schools where the participants shared the information gained with the rest of the teachers and
staff.

The first step in developing goals in each
school, according to Benjamin, was a thorough
evaluation of their current instructional program
and a comprehensive needs assessment. Effort was
made to enable everyone involved in the writing
process to understand exactly who decision-makers
are and how they utilized information gathered.
The tools used most in helping the educators
during the initial phase of evaluation were the
Evaluation Improvement Program materials developed
by the California State Department of Education.

Early in the school year Benjamin scheduled
the first series of three meetings with those
responsible for writing the Early Childhood
Education and Title I plans. During these initial
meetings Benjamin stressed the importance of
different kinds of testing materials such as
standardized and criterion-referenced tests in
gathering information critical to a thorough
evaluation.

179

The purpose of the second series of meetings was to assess needs by using data gathered during the evaluation period. During these meetings those responsible for writing the plans for the various schools shared with each other the different evaluative instruments they had developed. The participants rewrote and revised evaluation tools that needed alteration.

The final series of meetings was directed to the formulation of explicit goals and objectives. The participants were given practice in writing by first developing plans based on hypothetical data. Emphasis was placed on relating performance objectives directly to program goals and needs statements which included who learns or does what, when, under what conditions, at what minimum level, and how each will be measured.

Benjamin found that development of goals and objectives was the area needing most assistance. The California Evaluation Improvement Program materials were invaluable in helping the participants improve their expertise as project writers and program evaluators.

SKILLS FOR ETHICAL ACTION: A PROCESS APPROACH TO JUDGMENT AND ACTION

Chapman, Marian L. and Florence V. Davis.
Educational Leadership, Volume 35, March 1978, pp. 457-461.

Chapman and Davis describe the instructional program, Skills for Ethical Action, produced by Research for Better Schools, Inc., Philadelphia, Pennsylvania. Supported by funds from the National Institute of Education, the program has been tested and revised through the participation of 500 children and 14 teachers during a four-year period.

According to the authors, Skills for Ethical Action attempts to teach seventh and eighth grade students a process to make rational decisions about value questions in their lives. Efforts are made to raise students' levels of moral reasoning and to clarify their values. They are taught to link their values and moral reasoning to their behavior. The core of the program focuses on action taken after consideration is given to its effects on self and others. The six-step process called a "strategy" includes 1) identify the value question, 2) think up action ideas, 3) consider self and others, 4) judge, 5) act, and 6) evaluate.

The initial emphasis in Skills for Ethical Action instruction is on cognitive knowledge. Students learn basic definitions and the names and meanings of the process steps. They are required to practice using the six process steps by applying them to real situations in their own lives. Initially, the students identify the value that is involved in the situation. Once the value is identified they are encouraged to come up with many options that may be available. Then, the students think of possible consequences of their proposed actions on others and themselves. The students weigh those consequences to see if their proposed actions would be ethical and have a positive effect on every one concerned. Finally, the students are asked to commit themselves to actually carrying out the action they judged would be ethical.

Chapman and Davis do not see Skills for Ethical Action as the final answer to student judgment and action on moral and ethical issues, but rather as an effort to provide instruction in moral education's broad field. However, they note that students are pleased to find the ethicality of their proposed action and that repeated use of a strategy leads to improvement in the use of the steps.

ANOTHER LOOK AT INDIVIDUALIZED INSTRUCTION

Dunn, Rita. Phi Delta Kappan, Volume 59, February
    1978, pp. 400-402.

Dunn describes the development of an individualized instructional program in a newly
constructed elementary school of the Chappaqua
School System in Westchester County, New York.
Planning for the program began five months before
the Westorchard School opened in 1971. The
principal, Imogene St. Paul, urged the faculty to
develop a school-wide philosophy to express its
aims and objectives in the open space building.
Planning sessions with the faculty included an
August workshop followed by weekly sessions
throughout the school year.

The inservice program, according to Dunn,
provided sessions on mini-instructional centers,
carpentry, team teaching, record keeping, improving
student writing and math skills, and developing
contract activity packages. The staff development
program also included a two-week exchange of
faculty with teachers from several British primary
schools.

The author reports that the individualized
and open education program operated in Westorchard
has received extensive support from the community
and parents through their extensive participation
in development of programs, activities, assemblies,
trips, and other school concerns. Other services
that supported the faculty included instructional
specialists, high school students trained to
assist teachers, and part-time teacher aides.

Students are grouped according to age; however,
each child progresses at his own rate through large
and small groups or individualized instruction
utilizing multi-media approaches. To assist
students to learn, various tactics are employed
such as student free time for planning, individualized home work, inter-age projects, student councils,
a special "money" system that allows students to

earn and spend money for hobby items and services, a tutorial system, a lending zoo, a student operated post office, time for hobbies, and special programs during lunch and recess.

Dunn reports the first three years of the program at Westorchard were somewhat clouded by low achievement scores in reading and math compared to the other schools in the system. This led to citizen protests to the board of education resulting in the board and superintendent convening a special panel to evaluate the Westorchard program and make recommendations based on their findings. The panel of recognized educational leaders concluded that the school offered a very suitable and effective educational climate but that some practices needed improvement.

These recommendations for improvement stressed acclimating students to test-taking conditions and procedures. The school staff responded by simulating test conditions and concentrated on students working at longer periods of time without breaks, following directions precisely, and motivating students to take the tests seriously. The following year math and reading test scores for the Westorchard students improved significantly attaining scores higher than the other elementary schools in the school system and similar districts in the state and nation, based on data from the State of New York Pupil Evaluation Program.

Dunn concludes that students, parents, and teachers were pleased with the results of the individualized programs in an open space building. The Westorchard story is described as evidence that programs can be designed to teach the basics in reading and math through individualized instructional methods that stress individual learning styles and interests.

CURRICULUM DEVELOPMENT: A MODEL FOR ACTION

Eible, Charles V. and Joseph A. Zavarella.
NASSP Bulletin, Volume 63, March 1979,
pp. 85-90.

Eible and Zavarella report on a process for curriculum development, coordination, and evaluation in the Hendrick Hudson School District in New York. Embracing the concept that meaningful curriculum development involves all staff positions, a Curriculum Development Committee composed of teachers and administrators was formed. This committee defined guidelines for curriculum improvement which were adopted as policy by the school board.

Under these guidelines a Curriculum Review Committee was established to determine district curriculum priorities and to review proposals for curriculum changes. The committee was composed of one administrator, one elementary teacher, one middle school teacher, one high school teacher, one teacher-at-large, and the system-wide administrative assistant. This committee constructed a model for district-wide program reviews and curriculum changes with separate procedures for input by elementary, middle, and high schools. These procedures provide for involvement of persons at all levels of schooling. Each subject area committee, chaired by an elementary principal, is charged with responsibility in developing, implementing, evaluating, and revising curriculum in the specific subject areas.

Eible and Zavarella state that once a program is devised it is the principal's job to coordinate district-wide orientation in a specific area of learning. For example, the principal who is the chairperson of the math curriculum committee develops a math program across all elementary schools as well as the follow-through in middle and secondary levels. Also the teachers are involved at virtually all levels of the district's hierarchy with direct input for decision-making in curriculum matters.

Eible and Zavarella conclude that this process has brought about interest, involvement, and desirable results in the curriculum coordination problems at Hendrick School District. It has clarified the roles of administrators, school boards, and teachers in the total process of curriculum development and coordination.

TURNING IT AROUND IN EDUCATION WITH STUDENT TUTORING

Elliott, Arthur H. The Clearing House, Volume 50, March 1977, pp. 285-290.

Elliott describes a student tutoring program which improved student achievement in reading at the Soto Street School in Los Angeles. The program, "Programmed Tutoring in Reading," was directed by the school principal, Elbert Ebersole, over a period of six years during which time the school's average standardized reading test scores rose from considerably below average to definitely above average.

The author reports that the program began in 1966 when a special reading teacher experimentally assigned poor readers from the upper grades to assist less able first graders. As the upper grade tutors found they could actually read better than somebody else and when they were successful at helping younger students learn, their self-image improved as did the reading achievement of the first graders.

Elliott describes how the program spread so that within five years every child in the Soto Street School was involved as tutor, tutee, or both. A highly functioning tutoring structure has developed and procedures have been designed involving word study, word review, and reading phases. A kit also has been designed and is used by each tutor-tutee team as is a slide-tape sequence especially developed for training tutors. The training emphasis for the tutor is for developing a helping relationship with the tutee to assist in acquiring higher reading skill levels.

The author cites research studies which have confirmed the effectiveness of this program. He also reports on other research that confirms the use of tutors as an effective instructional procedure for helping students achieve cognitive, affective, and social development goals.

Elliott concludes that student tutoring is an instructional vehicle benefiting those involved that can readily be incorporated into any school or school system. Since the Soto Street School program has produced success over a period of six years and can be implemented through a systematized developmental approach by as few as four teachers, Elliott recommends it as a model for others to emulate.

HOW WE DEVELOP BILINGUAL INSTRUCTIONAL MATERIALS

Hartner, Eneida. Educational Leadership, Volume 35, October 1977, pp. 42-46.

Hartner reports on the operation of the Spanish Curricula Development Center (SCDC) located in Dade County, Florida, which since 1970 has been developing instructional materials for bilingual programs of Spanish and English. Presently, the Office of Bilingual Education in the U. S. Office of Education is supporting this center along with thirteen other selected centers.

The process of developing the materials began with assessing the needs of students, faculty, and community, consulting expert theorists and practitioners, and researching innovative and effective curricula. The philosophy resulting from that investigation is now being implemented in the "production of instructional materials in five basic areas or strands at the elementary level: Language Arts, Social Sciences, Science/Health,

Fine Arts, and Spanish as a Second Language." The materials in all areas except the last one are intended for native Spanish speakers and specifically target Mexican Americans or Chicanos, Puerto Ricans, and Cubans.

The curriculum established for the materials "was designed to be multi-disciplinary, integrated, and parallel, where necessary and cost-effective, to curricula existing in the regular school program." The actual content and structure of the material is controlled by a "Product Design" which was formulated for the purpose. It consists of a set of basic skills, concepts, and processes identified in the different disciplines and a set of "themes and concepts that serve as organizing threads for the entire curriculum" and "unify the different subject areas." Also included are "the main features, methods, techniques, and the general philosophy and rationale for the various approaches used in the curriculum" along with the "major goals for each strand." To fit the purpose of bilingual education, one of the goals in each strand, except Science/Health, along with developing the appropriate content and skills, is to present Hispanic experiences, tradition, and culture. Also, the main activities in the program are in Spanish.

Kits of instructional materials are produced for each grade level, containing a teacher's guide, visual supplements, a ditto packet, student texts, puppets, tape cassettes, and slides. Included with each unit are criterion-referenced tests to be used for placement, evaluation, and diagnoses. All the materials are field-tested with suggested revisions often being incorporated before the materials are released for general purchase. Various editions of kits for each level reflect regional and ethnic variations within the Hispanic culture. So far, materials are available for grades one through three in all five strands and for grades four through six in some of the strands.

The author claims that, according to tests

187

used in the experimental design for the Language
Arts Strand, "there is a significant difference
in achievement when students use SCDC materials."
He reports that users of the materials have not
only found them to be effective academically but
pleasing to students. They are in use by districts
in more than half the states.

CURRICULUM REVISION IN THE BIG CITY - MONEY VS.
    SENSE

Larkin, Martha M. The Clearing House, Volume 52,
    October 1978, pp. 89-93.

    Larkin describes an "all out" effort in a
large inner city Chicago high school to effect
curriculum revision and renewal. This change
program was determined as necessary because of
the high cutting of classes and failure rate
among the 3500 students.

    The unusual aspect of this problem is that
the school involved is a new multi-million dollar
nine story building that resulted from an intense
five year plan that included extensive preservice
for the staff. No expense had been spared in
the construction of the building or the provision
of resources for the new school. It contains such
features as air-conditioning, complete carpeting,
separate labs for special subjects, completely
equipped auto mechanics and electronic shops, a
computer terminal, a media center, open classrooms,
resource centers, a complete professional library,
radio and television studios, and operates through
modular and flexible scheduling.

    The author reports that the preservice
program included days for the staff to visit
other metropolitan high schools, extra inservice
days to allow for central office consultants to
offer advice and demonstrations, and culminated
with a four day workshop conducted by a national
consultant firm concerning team teaching,
individualizing instruction, and learning

activity packages. Teachers were paid for their involvement in these activities,and the climate was one of excitement and challenge.

When school began, it became obvious that these conditions did not contribute to educational gains, but in fact decreases were noted. The problems were then turned over to the school itself by the central administration. The author, who was serving as an assistant principal, was given charge to effect change.

Larkin describes steps taken for bringing about change and new programs. Two newly granted positions were created to assist in these efforts. For these positions two reliable teachers from the existing staff were selected and were assigned reading as the first priority. A curriculum committee of 30 members was formed whose agenda focused on needs assessment and development of goals and objectives. The function of each member was delineated with emphasis placed on using problem solving methods. Subcommittees were organized to use a designated procedure for dealing with problems. Faculty members and students were encouraged to submit new programs/courses to the school curriculum committee which was responsible for approving such programs on a pilot basis for one year. Curriculum specialists and coordinators worked with committees as requested and stressed individualized instruction throughout.

Larkin surmises that successes they have now come from within and are the responsibility of those involved. If given the chance, teachers will respond with dedication and hard work to bring about curriculum change. The experience demonstrated clearly to the author that the provision of physical plant, albeit at great expense, is futile unless teachers are given responsibility and involvement in the process of problem solving.

OPEN SPACE, OPEN EDUCATION, AND PUPIL PERFORMANCE

Lukasevich, Ann and Roland F. Gray. The Elementary
    School Journal, Volume 79, November 1978,
    pp. 108-113.

In an effort to determine the effect of
instructional style and architectural design on
pupil outcomes, Lukasevich and Gray reviewed fifty-
seven studies on open space schools and fourteen
studies on open education. They then conducted
their own study of five open space schools and
five traditionally built schools in the metropolitan area of Vancouver, Canada.

Findings from the studies of open space
schools revealed that nineteen favored open space
schools, eleven favored self-contained schools
with findings of twenty-seven being insignificant.
The studies on open education showed that three
favored open education, three favored non-open
education, and seven reported nonsignificant
findings. The researchers found that none of
these studies treated the variables of architectural style separately and failed to control
other significant variables.

Seeking to overcome the limitations of the
studies reviewed, they selected for study five
open space schools and five traditionally built
schools in the metropolitan area of Vancouver,
Canada. The schools were chosen on the basis of
openness of instruction in grades 1, 2, and 3 as
identified by thirteen criteria important in open
education programs. Third grade students taught
for two years in instructional situations classified as open or as nonopen were the subjects of
study.

According to the authors "separate stepwise
regression analyses were performed to test five
significant differences between groups classified
by program and facility and their interaction with
each other and with intelligence, socio-economic
status, and sex." Findings indicated that there

190

were significant differences in reading comprehension and mathematics concepts favoring the nonopen programs. However, scores for convergent mental ability and social virtues were significantly better in the open education programs.

Conclusions of the authors were that "it appears that the conventional style has a significant effect on achievement in mathematics concepts and in reading," and "better self-concept in relation to school subjects was found when children were taught in open space classrooms." Due to unexplainable interaction found in the study, the authors suggest that an instructional program with a medium degree of openness may be the best type of instructional program to promote growth in self-concept.

THE CURRICULUM: PATCHWORK OR CRAZY QUILT?

McCutcheon, Gail. Educational Leadership, Volume 36, November 1978, pp. 114-116.

McCutcheon reports on a study of curriculum planning at local schools in an endeavor to determine the nature of curriculum designs and forces which led to such curriculum designs. In 1978 the author, three graduate assistants, and twelve teachers studied the curriculums of twelve elementary classrooms, the decisions leading to those curriculums, and various influences upon the decisions.

The author reports that most curriculums studied resembled a crazy quilt pattern rather than any consistent pattern, and there were marked discrepancies between the formal written curriculum promulgated at the central administrative level and that operational in the schools. A variety of societal factors such as the appeasement of community groups, legislative regulation, system-wide textbook adoption, and scheduling constraints are cited as forces that have a disrupting, at times contradictory, influence on the curriculum.

Teachers, in their attempts to resolve and
accommodate these forces, often compromise the
coherence of the curriculum. One result of
this scenario is that both teachers and community
groups become confused about the purposes of the
school.

McCutcheon calls for system-wide deliberation
and response to these problems. She argues that
involvement of people at all levels might facilitate understanding of the schools' goals. Furthermore, she writes that in-service programs and
teacher committee work might help to maintain a
global focus on school curriculum.

Finally, McCutcheon calls for research into
the sources of curriculum, the nature of planning,
and the development of understandings about school
goals. She provides an analysis of the factors
that cause school curricula to be disjointed and
lacking in coherence and emphasizes the need for
investigation of these factors at both the
theoretical and practical level.

OPEN EDUCATION AS AN IDEOLOGY

Myers, Donald A. and Daniel L. Duke. Educational
    Research, Volume 19, June 1977, pp. 227-235.

Myers and Duke report on the results of their
1976 visits to 122 public elementary schools
reportedly engaged in open education in New York
State. From their reading and observations the
authors identified 68 characteristics of the open
education movement. Through refinement and pilot
testing "at an innovative laboratory at a state
college," a list of 16 criteria emerged. The list
included criteria such as vertical and horizontal
grouping; use of corridors, grounds, and community;
creative room arrangements; high but productive
noise level; a sense of community between teachers;
and highly flexible organization of time. The
authors used these 16 criteria to rate the schools
they visited.

Myers and Duke discovered that, based on raw scores and direct observation, nine criteria appear to be most essential to open education. Three of these criteria received higher scores than the others -- instruction, affective environment, and horizontal grouping. Consequently, the authors conclude, organization alone cannot account for effective open education. The three criteria with the lowest scores were vertical grouping (which ranked at the bottom); required learning; and use of corridors, grounds, and community.

The authors' analysis of their findings suggests that open education appears to be more of an ideology than a practicable, workable method. Much of what open education espouses is really synonymous with "good" education. Therefore, like so many other ideologies, open education will probably fade from the educational scene within a decade. One of the reasons the authors cited for the failure of open education to become a well-defined system is that educators, although eager to adopt open education, have often done so without any clear idea of what it really is. Consequently, many schools claim to be using open education without any real changes in curriculum. Further findings from the authors' observations are that most teachers in open education schools appear competent and that they work harder than teachers in traditional classrooms.

Myers and Duke conclude that open education "will defy definition as a discrete concept" and that, although it is a "logically tenable ideology," it lacks "the army of extraordinary teachers, the knowledge of how changes can be effectively introduced, the broad-based active support of administrators and citizens, and the conceptual clarity to make it a realistic alternative for the average public school ". Finally, even though the future of open education appears dim, the authors stress the fact that students were generally "active, happy, verbal, and interested in the

activities in which they were engaged." Furthermore, the teachers were competent and vitally
concerned with their students' progress.

THE GREENSVILLE PROGRAM: A COMMONSENSE APPROACH
TO BASICS

Owen, Samuel A. and Deborah L. Ranick. Phi Delta
Kappan, Volume 58, March 1977, pp. 531-539.

In 1972 students in the Greensville County,
Virginia school system ranked in the bottom
third of the nation on the Science Research
Associates Achievement Tests. Consequently,
Greensville County's educators decided to initiate
some radical changes to reverse the trend of
declining test scores and increasing numbers of
barely literate graduates - students who had for
years been socially promoted. Owen and Ranick
report on these changes and their dramatic results.

At the beginning of the 1973-74 academic year,
students and parents were told that there would be
no more social promotions and that every student
would be required to take a standardized achievement test twice a year. At the end of the year,
1300 of Greensville County's 3,750 students were
retained in grade. After meetings with parents
500 of these students were promoted. These were
students whose report cards indicated that they
had been doing satisfactory work up to this time.
From then on, however, no student has been
promoted unless the results of his or her achievement tests indicate that the student is functioning
at grade level.

According to the authors, each teacher is
responsible for evaluating his/her own students
based on teacher-made tests, recitations, and,
of course, a variety of standardized tests such
as the SRA Achievement Tests and the Iowa Tests
of Educational Development. To solve the problem
of retained pupils who would be older than their
classmates, Greensville County places the retained

students in classrooms with students their own age
where they receive a tailored instructional program. Students who can master some required skills
but not others are given partial promotion.
Teachers strive to create an environment of
success by letting their students know that they
believe they can succeed and that they expect
them to succeed.

Three important curriculum developments in
the secondary curriculum are the block schedule,
various levels of courses, and an alternative
program for students not interested in pursuing
academic subjects. The block schedule means that
the school day is divided into three periods,
each class lasting for one hour and 50 minutes.
This schedule eliminates wasted time and allows
students to concentrate on fewer subjects. Along
with advanced courses offered to college-bound
students, there are "practical" courses for those
students who require more time to master academic
skills, but no student is locked into one type of
course. For those students who prefer not to take
academic subjects, there is an Occupational
Proficiency Training Program, but a student must
be at least 14 years old and functioning two or
more grade levels behind the norm to qualify for
this program. Upon completion of this course, a
student receives a certificate of occupational
proficiency.

The results, reported by Owen and Ranick, of
Greensville County's new program are encouraging.
The dropout rate has decreased from 121 to 91 in
three years' time. The number of students having
to repeat a full grade has dropped to 268, achievement test scores have risen on all grade levels
so that students now rank in the top 50-60%, and
measured IQs have risen considerably. Students,
teachers, and the community at large are strongly
behind the innovations.

AN ALTERNATIVE TO THE CLASSROOM: TRAVEL FOR CREDIT

Przeklasa, Anthony, John Colombe, and John T.
     Rutkowski. The Clearing House, Volume 52,
     October 1978, pp. 76-77.

The authors report on a school sponsored
travel program implemented for students to develop
basic social studies and language arts skills.
For the past four years Argo Community High School
in Summit, Illinois, has provided an optional
educational experience for students to earn
curriculum credits through travel both in and out
of the United States. Trips have been taken to
such places as Spain, Yugoslavia, Italy, North
Africa, and Washington during which time nearly
three hundred students have developed awareness
of other cultures and shared their experiences
utilizing communication skills.

Participating students must complete seven
activities: 1) develop a preliminary research
project surveying the history, geography, politics,
customs, and economy of the country to be visited;
2) maintain a travel diary of what is experienced;
3) collect and organize travel artifacts; 4) write
a report on two significant sights; 5) develop a
two to three page paper concerning the leader of
the government in the country visited; 6) complete
a four to five page evaluation of the people of
the country based on direct experiences; and
7) write a critique of the travel program as a
means of learning.

Reasons given by the authors for implementing
the program are that experience is the best teacher;
there is little or no cost to the taxpayers
(students pay their own expenses); little classroom
space is needed; community involvement is prompted
through parent and alumni participation in the
program; there are economic travel opportunities
through group rates; and teacher-student rapport
is enhanced during travel time together. Travel
learning experiences were also suggested as

possibly becoming a part of the future life-style of students through their involvement in this program.

The authors advise that pragmatic procedures be followed to eliminate school liability which includes use of legal assistance to develop release forms and waivers for parents to sign and for student regulatory behavior guidelines. Other suggestions for successful implementation of a similar type program are that experienced travelers be used as chaperones and that constant communication be maintained between program participants and parents before, and especially during, the travel portion of the program.

The authors conclude that the travel program provides a valuable curriculum option and that this type experience provides a high degree of understanding which assists students in developing world survival and communication skills. Since these are major objectives in the social studies and language arts curriculum, the authors surmise that the travel program is fulfilling basic needs and therefore is a valuable and accredited part of their school's program.

CITY EXPERIENCES FOR SUBURBAN HIGH SCHOOLS

Rooney, Jim and Doug Thompson. NASSP Bulletin, Volume 62, November 1978, pp. 94-101.

Rooney and Thompson describe programs they developed to familiarize suburban high school students with urban areas and to give them city experiences. These intense programs acquainted students of Mountain Open High School in Evergreen, Colorado with the City of Denver and students of Village School in Great Neck, New York with New York City.

The authors describe how they have organized their programs into three phases: 1) exploration - introducing students to the city, 2) focusing -

selecting targets or issues for intense study, and 3) action - motivating students to self-initiated projects and the tying together of issues. These programs have also involved a wide range of curriculum integration that includes sociology, architecture, consumer mathematics, art, photography, history, journalism, urban ecology, and social action.

During the exploration phase, students ride various public transportation routes, participate in "wilderness training," and form teams to locate certain places for which they must show proof of visiting. The activities of this phase have been observed by the authors to alleviate anxieties about large city settings and the helpless feelings caused by unfamiliar environment.

Rooney and Thompson describe the focusing phase of the programs as heavily involving human resources such as newspaper reporters to familiarize the students with different ethnic neighborhoods and other aspects of the city. During this phase students gain appreciation for the diversity of the populations within the city and their reasons for resisting homogenization.

The action phase stresses independent study and allows students to become involved in attacking problems and dealing with concerns. Such projects have resulted in students investigating politics, sociology, and ecology. They have also led students to conduct research and become involved in areas in which they have sustained interest for periods ranging over several years.

The authors report preparation as a key to success of these type programs. Many of the logistic problems need the support of the school administration and the parents as time away from school and home can amount to several consecutive days and nights. Student involvement includes planning arrangements for such things as logding, meals, and equipment. The hazards inherent in

this type program center around student safety
liability and the investment by teachers and
students in large amounts of time and finance.

Rooney and Thompson conclude that the city
experiences for suburban students are extremely
worthwhile in both curricular and extra-curricular achievement. They urge other schools to use
the type of experiences described in this article
only for motivation and as a guide for developing
their own programs.

WHAT IS THE STATUS OF STATE-FEDERAL RELATIONSHIPS
    IN SCHOOLING?

Singletary, H. Titus, Jr. Educational Leadership,
    Volume 35, February 1978, pp. 374-379.

Singletary reports on the relationship and
role of the state and federal government in schools
based on a survey of state department of education
representatives in several states. Specific
attention is given to the influence of the federal
government on curriculum and the changes this has
brought since 1960.

The author addresses the various influences of
the federal government beginning with citizenship
development. Next he notes that attention was
given to the development of leadership as the
states expanded West followed by the third emphasis
which was the nationwide effort to stimulate
vocational education. The launching of Sputnik
triggered an emphasis in the scientific, mathematics,
and diplomatic fields. The most recent federal
surge has been that of providing for and educating
groups with special needs.

Respondents to the survey expressed concern
for federal encroachment on decision-making through
controls accompanying federal aid. Positive
influences of the federal government on curriculum
most often expressed were enrichment of educational
opportunities for the disadvantaged, support of

199

individual education programs, major changes in course offerings, development of curriculum materials in mathematics, science, and languages, and a focus on needs assessment. Findings of the survey indicate that there is an absence of clear-cut policy on education at federal level, showing that education continues to be primarily a state responsibility.

In the past 20 years, Singletary says there has been a strengthening of state departments of education through federal assistance and a significant increase in money available for education with an accompanying movement toward educational accountability. Requests for more precise data on which to make decisions about appropriations have brought a more active involvement of the federal government in the day-to-day operation of schools. This, he says, has brought about conflict between state and federal control of education.

Singletary calls attention to national studies conducted by HEW on areas such as population, education, and the federal role; state programs in bilingual education; minimal competency education; and training educators for the handicapped. He says these national studies probably reflect emerging ideas for federal influence. Movements such as these studies indicate the increasing need for a national policy on education generated by a system which enhances and supports efforts of state and local school districts.

OPTIONS IN HIGH SCHOOL DISCIPLINE

Sinner, Gregg and J. L. Sinner. Phi Delta Kappan, Volume 59, February 1978, pp. 407-409.

Sinner and Sinner discuss programs which one comprehensive, grades 9-12, 1,070-student regional high school in Vermont is providing to combat alienation and discipline problems among its students. In order to respond more to human need

and make the school less a factory and more a
family, seven specific programs that are alternatives to the traditional school offerings are
available to all students on a voluntary basis
in this Vermont school. The programs are DUO,
Boys' Life, Summer Challenge, Summer Site Betterment Project, Girls' Life, Peer Counseling, and
the Learning Place.

DUO ("Do Unto Others") is a program in which
high school students may earn credit toward
graduation for experiential learning in community
service and apprenticeship projects. Students
commit one-half or one day per week to their DUO
project and are responsible for the work they
miss in their regular classes.

Boys' Life is a self-contained, autonomous
program conducted in the local town hall offering
on-the-job training opportunities, remedial
instruction, and social interaction skills development. The program is operated throughout the year.

Summer Challenge is an Outward-Bound-like
experience involving school staff and community
representatives. The program combines rigorous,
stressful outdoor physical training and experience
with vocabulary building and writing skills
development.

The Summer Site Betterment Project involved
college students and high school students in
betterment of their own school sites. This was
a single mid-summer project which could become a
year-round project. The students painted murals,
planted trees, and constructed a greenhouse. Also,
the students worked on their writing skills by
keeping journals. Most important of all, the
students were involved in their school.

Girls' Life Program (counterpart of Boys'
Life) provides similar opportunities for young
women. It emphasizes awareness and skills in the
practical areas of child care, nutrition, money
management, and in legal rights and resources.

Peer Counseling, based on the notion that most young people are willing to discuss real concerns with peers more readily than with adults, provides opportunities for students to help each other.

The Learning Place, a program in which students have a significant say in program design, staff selection, evaluation, and governance, centers around the democratic process. The program was conceived by a group of community people concerned about non-achievers and under-achievers. The program involves a strong counseling component, academic and experiential learning, and use of the community as a learning resource.

Sinner and Sinner state that many of the youngsters who have chosen or will choose these programs would otherwise probably not have survived in the Vermont school system. Discipline problems would probably be substantially worse were the programs not available. They conclude that these programs provide better communication with the community and more responsiveness in education by caring for the "turned off" and "turned-out" students, and help relieve some discipline problems which stem directly from the failure of the school to respond to human need.

OTHER REFERENCES

Bock, Daniel R. "Summerhill Is Alive and Well,"
Educational Leadership, Volume 35, February
1978, pp. 380-383.

Brown, Margarette and Judy Singleton. "Teaching
LD Adolescents," Today's Education, Volume 66,
November-December 1977, pp. 43-46.

Calhoun, George Jr. and Raymond N. Elliott, Jr.
"Self Concept and Academic Achievement of
Educable Retarded and Emotionally Disturbed
Pupils," Exceptional Children, Volume 43,
March 1977, pp. 379-380.

Chiang, Alice. "The Computer Lends a Helping
Hand," Audiovisual Instruction, Volume 24,
May 1979, p. 28.

Cohen, Milton. "Adult Students in Public School
Classes," The Clearing House, Volume 52,
February 1979, pp. 272-275.

Cordisco, Jane Hunt. "Community-based Learning
in the Secondary School," Educational Leadership, Volume 36, April 1979, pp. 493-496.

DeRoche, Edward F. and Jules J. Modlinski.
"Commando Academy: From Clashes to Classrooms,"
Educational Leadership, Volume 34, March 1977,
pp. 429-432.

Dykman, Ruth Anne. "In Step with 94-142, Two by
Two," Music Educators Journal, Volume 65,
January 1979, pp. 58-63.

Ford, Bonny E. "Multiage Grouping in the Elemen-
tary School and Children's Affective Development:
A Review of Recent Research," Elementary School
Journal, Volume 78, November 1977, pp. 149-159.

Gough, Pauline B. "Television Takes a Turn at
Essential Learning Skills," Phi Delta Kappan,
Volume 59, June 1978, pp. 672-673.

Hassett, John J. "Bilingual Teaching for Newly Arrived Immigrant Children," The Clearing House, Volume 50, May 1977, pp. 409-412.

Hodges, Walter L., Robert Sheehan, and Harry Carter. "Educational Intervention: The Role of Follow Through Sponsors," Phi Delta Kappan, Volume 60, May 1979, pp. 666-669.

Lipman, Victor. "The Alternative School Capital of the World," American Education, Volume 14, December 1978, pp. 33-36.

Lockard, Geraldine. "Mainstreaming: One Child's Experience," Phi Delta Kappan, Volume 59, April 1978, pp. 527-528.

Massie, Dorothy. "Update on Education of the Handicapped," Today's Education, Volume 67, September-October 1978, pp. 60-62, 73.

Morrill, Leslie Tierney. "S.C.A.P.E. From Stigma: Will Your Middle School Be Ready for P.L. 94-142?" The Clearing House, Volume 52, May 1979, pp. 456-457.

Moynahan, Terry. "Vocational Education and the Handicapped," Today's Education, Volume 69, April-May 1979, pp. 47-48.

Nourse, Bartley B. Jr. "Students Exploring Alternative Life-Styles," Phi Delta Kappan, Volume 60, February 1979, pp. 448-451.

Puig, Hiram H. "Puerto Rico Experiments with College Courses by Television," Phi Delta Kappan, Volume 60, June 1979, pp. 723-724.

Yates, Janie B. "A New Alternative School: CEEC," The Clearing House, Volume 52, February 1979, pp. 265-271.

CHAPTER IX
ORGANIZATIONAL STRUCTURES

The common school usually referred to as
kindergarten through high school has long been
the framework for education of America's children.
Throughout the history of this institution various
forms of organization have been devised to
accommodate the varying ages of children and
levels of instruction. Some of the earliest
structures are known as dame school, Latin-grammar
school, academy, and college. More recently the
span of educational organization is covered by
the terms early childhood education, middle
school, secondary school, junior college, and
university. Within this framework and cutting
across it, numerous structures may be found. The
concerns and special interests of educators and
the general public are expressed most often in
forms such as special education, vocational/
technical education, numerous alternative schools,
and a variety of instructional management systems.

Change or modification of the school's
organizational structures seems the most accessible
means for coping with the ills of failing students,
placating disgruntled parents and those with
special ambitions for their off-springs, and
responding to the concerns of taxpaying citizens.
Private and parochial schools have long been the
haven for the elitists and those with special
religious commitments. Solutions to sociological
problems, more especially identified as racial
and minority discrimination, sought through the
common schools have sponsored innumerable
organizational structures. All kinds of private
institutions have sprung up mostly under the guise
of college preparatory and special religious
commitment institutions. It may be said that the
chief force behind the rapid development of the
middle school and flux of private schools is
federal pressures to integrate the common schools.

205

The rapid expansion of cities and urbanization of rural areas have created challenging environmental problems which have strained school organizational structures, facilities, and financial systems to the breaking point. Educational remedies brought forth by these factors are decentralization, consolidation, and coordination among school systems through cooperative educational service agencies (CESA). Efforts to equalize educational opportunities among neighborhood schools, make education more attractive and effective, and to speed desegregation have resulted in development of educational plazas, parks or multischools, and comprehensive secondary schools. At the same time, large school systems are being decentralized,and the power to govern is being delegated to responsible groups in districts within a school system. Particular attention is being given to special subject emphases organizations known as magnet schools.

Organizational structures which give special attention to the vocational/technical aspects of education are being given high priority. Educators and the public now realize that the traditional concept of college is not necessary nor desirable for everyone. The high rate of secondary school drop-outs has caused educators to reevaluate the educational process in relation to structures which provide for vocational/technical education. It is now realized that education for the technical secretary, cosmetologist and computer technician must find its place along with that of the physician and art critic. According to the proponents of vocational/technical education, a structure which provides for varied laboratory experiences, field trips, and on-the-job training is as necessary as the lecture hall and the library.

The demands for education of all youth, triggered by the Educational Policies Commission in the 1930's and 1940's, began to be felt in the 1950's through individual state allotments of special education teachers. Growth in state and federal budgets for all forms of special education since 1950 is phenomenal. Federal legislation within the last decade mandates not only education for all handicapped children, special needs cases, and the gifted, but requires that physical barriers to the accessibility of educational facilities be removed. Today exceptional children comprise a large percentage of youth in the common schools. These include the physically handicapped, educable mentally retarded, learning disabled, gifted, economically and culturally disadvantaged, and many other special classifications of exceptionality. Realizing that persons in these classifications needed special attention,a whole new framework of education sprang up alongside of and in the building with the regular instruction of the common schools.

Initially,special education meant that special teachers for children according to their classified exceptionalities were assigned to separate space with modified curriculum and selected resources and instructional materials. This original pattern of placing children in groupings and/or in separate learning areas created an environment not necessarily conducive to the maximum stimulation for learning. Acting upon the findings that exceptional children learn most when placed in learning areas with the rank and file of all children, federal legislation mandated the mainstreaming - placement in regular classrooms - of exceptional children where at all feasible. This stance assumes that strict attention be given to diagnostic identification of the capabilities and needs of all children and that individual educational prescriptions direct the learning experiences of those with special needs.

The availability of federal financing has encouraged more local boards of education to take a fresh look at these exceptional students who were dealt with in the past as a problem rather than a challenge. Many areas of specialization have more money and resources at present than were ever available in the past. Given the current emphasis on compensatory education for exceptional children, there is probably no community of any size that is

not providing many special services to this select
population in our schools.

Although no one best method of educating
exceptional students has been found, the search
for better methods continues on a nationwide basis.
Generally the areas in which programs for exceptional students are being developed are those of
teacher recruitment and training, curricular
innovation, parental involvement, and community
assistance and involvement.

A growing awareness on the part of educators
and the provision of more money and resources for
exceptional children have forged a new emphasis
in education. Curriculum experiences, programs,
and activities, designed to compensate for the
deprivation of exceptional children and youth, are
being implemented. These programs are playing a
vital part in assisting this sizable percentage of
America's school population as well as making
better provision for all other youth.

Education may be said to provide effectively
for each student when content, concepts, materials,
and processes are appropriate for each learner, the
pacing is geared to each individual, and the depth
or breadth of the encounter meets the interests
and needs of each one involved. The complex
society of today causes each individual to cope
with a wide range of competition for his time and
energies. It necessitates individual ability to
inquire, to seek, to discover, to modify, and to
invent. Just to memorize, to store up, and to be
able to understand, comprehend, sensitize, and
regenerate is not enough. Each person must use
all the skills, tools, and resources possible in
order to be in command of him/herself and master
of whatever situations and conditions are encountered.

The school therefore must provide organizational structures which give consideration to the
individual's interests, talents, intelligence,
achievement, cognitive style, motor perceptual

capabilities, social development, learning skills, set for learning, personality, motivation, moral codes, and scope of values. A wide variety of instructional management systems have been developed to cope with this tremendous responsibility of educators. Among those systems most readily recognized are: individually prescribed instruction (IPI), programmed learning according to needs (PLAN), individually guided education (IGE), handicapped education learner planning system (HELPS), and the many adaptations of computer assisted instruction (CAI).

Computer assisted instruction is an organizational structure capable of harboring the most comprehensive educational program,yet sensitive enough to serve as an individual tutor where questions and answers are exchanged by student and (teacher) computer. The computer can be programmed to assist in the preparation of simulated problems or present a different approach to learning a specific concept. Major objectives attained through CAI are assessment of individual differences in the development of subject matter, development of self-directed learners, and opportunity for actual involvement. The computer places the teacher in the roles of student counselor, coordinator of systems components, and sculptor for instructional design and strategy.

A complete instructional management system provides random access/retrieval for specific information on specified topics and subjects, video tapes, interactive computer-assisted instruction, visual communication, a school-wide closed circuit television network, and a cumulative record of student progress in learning activities. CAI has the capability of interrelating student based psychoeducational data with educational objectives, instructional activities, curriculum materials, and supportive information for teaching a given group in a specified learning area. It may feature a diagnostive-prescriptive instructional program using flexible grouping patterns to provide for instructional grouping, needs groups, and individual instruction.

Although organizational structures cannot provide for the concerns of all who look to the schools to prepare for the needs of society, they do make it possible for adjustments to be made. The basic organizational vertical groups have changed very little. Change of the junior high school to middle school in many locations and the addition of the tremendous structure of special education are the changes most obvious. Other fast developing organizational patterns are technical schools and comprehensive high schools which provide many additional career related offerings. The most recent movement is that of early childhood education programs. This encompasses several versions of compensatory programs and effects the lowering of entrance age into organized education for children. The focus of the current efforts toward changed structures is that of providing more effective learning opportunities for all ages.

SYNOPSES

A LOOK AT BILINGUAL PROGRAMS IN DADE COUNTY:
GATEWAY TO THE LATIN WORLD

Bequer, Marta M. Educational Leadership, Volume
      35, May 1978, pp. 644-648.

Bequer describes the bilingual programs
offered by the Dade County Public Schools in
Florida. The magnitude of the need for such a
program is evident as this geographic area contains
500,000 people of Hispanic origin with the schools
enrolling over 25,000 students who speak English as
a second language and therefore need special
instruction. Spanish is the predominant language
among these students, however Haitian, Vietnamese,
and other languages are also dominant in many
homes.

Miami, located in Dade County, is also host
to thousands of Latin American visitors each year.
The total effect of these large numbers of Spanish
speaking people being present has created a demand
for English speaking people to learn the Spanish
language; therefore, the schools provide instruction in Spanish to everyone who desires it.

The author reports that to supplement local
financing of bilingual programs, Dade County
receives aid from various federal and state sources
in the form of funded projects. The resulting
programs are for language maintenance or transition
serving all kinds of children utilizing teachers
who are as varied in type as the students they
instruct.

One of the projects the author describes is
the Elementary and Secondary Education Act (ESEA)
Bilingual which provides support for staff development, staffing, and instructional materials. A
component of this project is a systems management
approach to reading in Spanish that develops skills
involving decoding and comprehension within a

211

diagnostic-prescriptive approach. This project produces materials for teacher training, pre and post tests, selective diagnostic tests, individual and group profiles, and instructional materials that include designs for learning centers.

Bequer also discusses the Spanish Curriculum Development Center (SCDC) which produces curriculum materials organized into units and kits unifying the curriculum. One of the components of this program teaches Spanish language and Latin Culture to the English speaking blacks and Anglos.

A third project reported is Individualized Spanish for Speakers of English (ISSE). The staff of this project have created and developed seventeen books to assist students in learning Spanish. Cassette tapes accompany the books which deal with vocations, Spanish expressions relating to customs of Spanish speaking people, and language vocabulary and patterns to facilitate communication in eight areas of the world.

The fourth project described by Bequer is "Bilingual Alternative to Secondary Education" which provides guidance activities for students, conversational units for counselors and administrators, training modules for counselors, informational units for parents on school organization-functioning, and units on cultural differences. The goal of this project is to establish better communication and understanding between the school and the family which will hopefully result in more relevant and better school programs.

Bequer concludes that Dade County Schools recognize that education is the key to future ethnic and racial harmony. This position is supported through the variety and amount of programs and projects the system operates to equip all students with the bilingual tools to allow them to function in our multicultural society.

212

A ROLE FOR COMPUTERS IN INDIVIDUALIZING EDUCATION -
AND IT'S NOT TEACHING

Dagnon, Carol and Dennis W. Spuck. Phi Delta
    Kappan, Volume 58, February 1977, pp. 460-462.

    Dagnon and Spuck report the use of Computer
Managed Instruction (CMI) in a project sponsored
by the Research and Development Center for Cognitive
Learning in Madison, Wisconsin to support their
program of Individually Guided Education (IGE).
This program which necessitates specified and
measurable instructional objectives, levels of
mastery for each specific objective established,
and criterion-referenced tests and/or observation
schedules to assess achievement is operable in
several situations. Among the situations in
Wisconsin using CMI are the Wisconsin System of
Instructional Management in seven communities
involving more than 2,500 students; three individualized programs involving math, reading, and
science; and eight schools using computers with
their reading program.

    Dagnon and Spuck report that all of these
programs use the computer to store and process
student achievement data gained from formal tests
and teacher observations. Print-outs on these
data are made available through school based
terminals within thirty minutes. Three kinds of
reports needed by teachers for instructional
decisions in this individualized program which
can be managed by the computer are achievement
profiles, diagnostic reports, and grouping
recommendations.

    Achievement profiles show progress of an
individual or group of students concerning several
objectives. These reports are used in classrooms
for feedback to students showing their progress
and by teachers for reporting to parents via
conference or report cards.

    Diagnostic reports compare actual performance
with expectations. The computer locates and flags

students who need special help diagnosed from input data. Other data generated indicate expectations that may need to be revised, instructional activities being used that are failing to teach the intended objectives, and skills areas needed for each student.

Grouping recommendations from the computer are 1) listings of students ready for those objectives selected to next be taught, 2) lists of students eligible for more than just one of the selected objectives, and 3) lists of students not qualifying for any of the objectives because of existing mastery or lack of necessary prerequisite knowledge. These types of grouping reports eliminate much teacher and/or aide time and are sometimes the basis for forming additional groups, individual study units, and alternative learning situations.

Dagnon and Spuck report that use of the computer in this type system allows schools to continuously monitor and adjust their instructional program. School managers can analyze and evaluate school and district progress concerning particular curricula at any point in time. Instructional materials and strategies for objectives and topics can also be reviewed for effectiveness. They conclude that teachers are not replaced in critical functions by computer use, but are assisted by receiving immediate information they can use for truly important functions such as diagnosing and prescribing. These are the critical processes through which the computer can offer an effective and organized program.

AN INDIVIDUALIZED TYPEWRITING PROGRAM

Gades, Robert E. and Birdie H. Holder. Journal of Business Education, Volume 53, May 1978, pp. 338-339.

The authors describe an individualized type-writing program which established its superiority over traditional methods of instruction and class organization at the University of Nebraska, Lincoln. The designer determined to make this individualized program more than the usual continuous progress or independent learning program. The instructional plan utilized data on student abilities and relevant background for determining initial entry in the program. The evaluation system was designed to discriminate and report specific abilities and skills such that adjustments could be made periodically in order for the individual to master all phases of the course at a minimum competency level.

Students are introduced to the typewriting program and given a placement test during the first week to assess each student's competence in typewriting. This provides data for placing individual students at different points in each of the production areas (letters, manuscripts, tabulations, and business forms). Program materials including a general handbook, a keyboard presentation and skill development booklet, and eighteen individual production units are used to guide and facilitate the individual. Unique to this program is an accompanying set of sound-on-slides carefully coordinated with the regular tested materials which students are directed to view before typing each program area.

Students in the University of Nebraska program are enrolled in a specific class taught by a single instructor. This person gives timed writings, administers and grades post tests, conducts drills, and assists students with materials or media according to individual needs. The instructor continuously encourages students and conducts ongoing evaluation of the program.

The authors report favorable evaluation of the typing program based on findings of an external evaluator and responses of students and faculty. Statements of appraisal as compared to traditional programs show 1) students' grades are equal or

215

better, 2) speed and accuracy are equal or better,
3) less time is required to complete a semester's
work, and 4) students preferred the individualized
approach.

OUTDOOR EDUCATION CAN HELP THE HANDICAPPED

Hedberg, Sally. Today's Education, Volume 69,
    April-May 1980, pp. 54, 55, 83.

Organizational changes to accommodate 13
severely disabled students brought new expereinces
to Miramonte High School, Orinda, California.
Hedberg shares some of the more trying and exciting
encounters that resulted from integrating these
handicapped students into regular classrooms.
Generally, the handicapped students were able to
cope with the academics with some extra help, but
the matter of relating to other students posed a
severe problem. Several organized activities
were developed to accommodate this need, but the
main feature was participation in a Yosemite
Institute, an independent, nonprofit environmental
education organization.

This outdoor education program for disabled
students in Yosemite National Park served as the
incentive for helping the disabled students gain
confidence in relating to others. Participation
in several projects such as organizing a club,
forming groups to attend school games and dances,
eating with others at lunch, and entering a float
at Homecoming paved the way for the week long
institute.

Preparation for the institute involved the
participation of parents in viewing a slide show
about the Institute and other activities to develop
student and parent readiness for this trip of the
students away from home. Since there were many
high school groups at Yosemite, counselors and
guides were specifically informed as to the nature
and limitations of the disabled students.

216

Once at the camp the students of Miramonte
participated in the regular activities of common
meals and camp program activities. The leaders
of this particular group adapted the Institute's
regular outdoor education program to fit these
students' needs, providing opportunities for them
to take risks -- a valuable aspect of the program--
which the disabled accepted as a challenge.
Mountain climbing and skiing, at their own pace,
were punctuated with rest stops at which stories
of famous naturalists were read. The Yosemite
experience built confidence and skills helpful
to the students later in backpacking and river
rafting.

Hedberg recounts with pride not only the
accomplishments of the handicapped students but
the change in attitude toward more acceptance of
them by faculty and other students. She says
these once withdrawn students now communicate
more freely. Counselors, the psychologist, special
teachers, and therapists give their support to the
disabled and their classroom teachers. They now
provide experiences to supplement their social and
emotional growth previously not considered.

THE WORTH OF THE FOLLOW THROUGH EXPERIENCE

Hodges, Walter L. Harvard Educational Review,
     Volume 48, May 1978, pp. 186-192.

Hodges reports successful findings, based on
"a careful review of Follow Through and its
evaluations," made on this compensatory-education
program. Citing (and often challenging) data from
studies such as the one by House, Glass, McLean,
and Walker in 1978 and the one by Stebbins,
St. Pierre, Anderson, Proper, and Cerva in 1977;
Hodges shows that Follow Through "in many important
areas, including academic achievement ... was
successful."

Hodges challenges conclusions drawn from

217

evaluations made on Follow Through programs used
to report to the President of the United States
that results of the Program were "not positive
enough to justify continued preferential treatment."
Errors cited that could have made the difference
in the overall program include 1) numerous sampling
and methodological problems, 2) narrowness of the
evaluator's perspective, and 3) uncritical acceptance of the belief that the traditional experimental model in evaluation research should be
approximated at all cost. The author is strongly
critical that only those data that fit the
traditional model were utilized. He seems
convinced that "if Follow Through is completely
and properly analyzed, it can become the most
instructive educational study ever done in this
country." Sources cited as yielding more positive
data are local school districts, sponsors' offices,
and voluminous reports submitted to the United
States Office of Education (USOE) by research
contractors.

Hodges' conclusions as to the successfulness
of Follow Through are supported by seven specific
examples generated during the use of the Program.
First, national evaluation achievement data are
much more encouraging when compared directly with
national math and reading norm data. Second,
school district sites had results in keeping with
the goals of the models implemented. Third,
parent interest in the schools and in their
children's education was increased when volunteers
in school activities among parents in Follow
Through doubled. Fourth, sponsors documented
claims that Follow Through made schools and homes
happier. Fifth, a number of relatively comprehensive models for primary education were developed
and demonstrated. "Thus, the Follow Through
program has served as a kind of curriculum - and
instrument - development laboratory." Sixth, a
new model for tying theory and research to
educational practice was developed. And seventh,
a new avenue for the improvement of teaching with
more effective supervision and accountability was
opened.

OUR SKILLS CENTER'S SUCCESS

Hodgson, Barbara. Today's Education, Volume 67,
April-May 1978, pp. 63-64.

Hodgson describes the success of the Owen C.
Sabin Occupational Skills Center, North Clackamas
School District, Milwaukie, Oregon. Since 1968
this facility has provided its graduates with job
entry skills and the ability to secure and maintain a job. It has also provided for all students
in the area (vocational and academic) the opportunity to become acquainted with a variety of
occupations through direct experience and informal
contact with surrounding job clusters.

In 1968 the District secured $385,000 from
the Vocational Education Act of 1963 with the
proceeds of a three-year serial levy to establish
the Skills Center. Today twelve job clusters
provide on-hands training for approximately 1,000
high school students. They are agricultural
production, building construction, child services,
electricity and electronics, graphic reproduction,
industrial mechanics, metals, data processing,
health occupations, marketing and management,
nursery/landscaping, and forest products.

Hodgson credits the Center's success to the
composition of the teaching staff who are experienced craftspersons and professionals who develop
the concept of "how to work" along with the
teaching of safety habits, care of equipment, the
importance of productivity, and responsibility on
the job. Students learn on the job skills while
producing a usable product such as a house, a
vacation home, or buildings on the Skills Center
campus itself. Through these experiences they
develop mutually beneficial relationships with the
industrial and business community of the Portland
metropolitan area. This relationship with the
community has developed into twelve advisory
committees composed of local business and trades
people who help with curriculum and practices for

each job cluster. Local businesses donate equipment and provide job opportunities; the Skills Center provides hundreds of trained graduates ready to go to work.

Hodgson cites several success cases of graduates, such as, Jay McAlonen, a graduate from the graphic reproduction cluster, who got a job and started his own business and in turn hired Skills Center graduates. McAlonen states that he holds "a job I never would have gotten without my classes at the Skills Center."

Follow-up studies of Skill Center graduates from 1972-75 show that six months after graduation at least half are studying or employed in areas closely related to the job cluster they pursued at the Center. Of the responding graduates from 1975, 58.2 percent were in cluster-related post high school activities--half in jobs and half in two or four year institutions.

Hodgson concludes that the Skills Center has fulfilled its dual role of providing its graduates with job entry skills and job holding capability and acquainting other students with a variety of occupational experience and informal contact with surrounding clusters.

CONCORD HIGH: AN EXPERIMENT IN INTENSIVE EDUCATION

Keller, Arnold J. The Clearing House, Volume 52, November 1978, pp. 119-121.

Keller describes an attempt by the Concord High School, located on New York City's Staten Island, to implement an intensive education program. This 19th Century vintage school lacks facilities usually associated with innovative programs such as media center, well equipped labs, and other modern conveniences. However, it does house an alternative education program offering an opportunity for students, faculty, and administration to be involved in an unprecedented approach to public schooling.

The author reports that the intensive education program is developed around the concept that students can learn better when concentrating on one subject at a time. This "back to basics" alternative school features four 45 day cycles within a school year. During each cycle, students study one major subject for three and one-half hours each day intertwined with social studies, a learning community activity, and lunch. As the cycles change, so do the main subjects which consist of English, science, math, and foreign language. The learning community activity provides small group work utilizing individualized learning packages as an alternative that supplements the intense study of the main subject.

Keller reports the grading system consists of the students earning competency credits based on achievement levels rather than Carnegie units. Thus, their diploma reflects mastery of knowledge as measured by the New York State Regents examination and teacher-made tests rather than attendance and passing grades in subject based classes. Students can also be partially recycled at Concord High in an intensive subject for more complete mastery learning.

The author describes additional features of this program as options for students to participate in "great book" seminars, student input on curriculum and other school operations, continual dialogue with parents through a highly interactive parent-teacher organization, and the implicit understanding among the faculty and administration that their success will depend on continuing team efforts and collaboration.

Keller reports that intensive education approaches to various curriculum courses are also underway at other schools such as: Gill/St. Bernard School, New Jersey; Cambridge School of Weston, Massachusetts; Phillips Academy of Andover, Massachusetts; Colorado College, Colorado Springs, Colorado; and Hiram College, Hiram, Ohio. A

majority of these schools report a major
advantage to having this type of program is the
relationships that result from students and
faculty working closely together during most of
every school day.

Keller concludes that he perceives the
Concord program causing things to happen for the
better, creating more responsiveness by the
faculty, and resulting in good student adjustment,
positive attitudes toward learning, a high rate
of student attendance, and few discipline problems.
Regardless of whether achievement levels of students in intensive education are higher or lower
than those in traditional programs, Keller stresses
that the real strength of such a school program
may well turn out to be establishment of warm
relationships by faculty and students.

EXTENDED DAY KINDERGARTEN

Mason, Barbara K. School and Community, Volume
    63, May 1977, pp. 28, 38.

Mason reports on the Kansas City Extended
Day Kindergarten plan. This program, sponsored
by the Title I Compensatory Program, provides 690
five-year olds in 17 schools with full day sessions
of kindergarten.

According to Mason each child in the school
district attends kindergarten all day until
October 1. During this time the Kindergarten
Individual Readiness Profile Pre-Test is given
to each child to determine which children are
eligible to continue in the all-day sessions. The
extended day classes are limited to 15 children.
These 15 children attend the regular half-day
session with the other children and then have the
extended session with the same teacher. The
extended day is designed to provide additional
assistance in reading readiness, communication
skills, and mathematics.

222

Special features which help to make the
program a success are learning centers, individual
progress reports, home learning kits, and learning
boxes. These materials provide independent
learning tasks for the children. In-service
training for teachers is a vital factor in enabling
teachers to make the program effective.

Mason concludes that children in Kansas City's
Extended Day Kindergarten profit from the extra
time based on reports of many success stories of
the program. A significant result of the program
has been the finding by teachers that extra time
spent with children at this early age can make
a significant difference in their educational
development. As a result of this success the
program has been cited as an exemplary program
by the Kansas State Department of Elementary and
Secondary Education.

MIDDLE SCHOOL EFFECTIVENESS: A THREE YEAR STUDY

McGee, Jerry C. and Robert J. Krajewski. Middle
     School Journal, Volume 10, November 1979,
     pp. 16-17.

McGee and Krajewski report on a three year
project designed to assist in the transformation
of the J.B. Brown Junior High School of Hamilton
County, Tennessee, to a middle school. Funded
through ESEA Title III, the project was monitored
two to three days each Spring by the authors as
a project evaluation team effort. This article
describes the results obtained by viewing the
total school program through 1) interviews with
parents, students, faculty, and the principal;
2) planning sessions and classroom and team
meetings; 3) review of schedules, programs,
materials, and guides; and 4) the collection and
analysis of data relating to the objectives.

The authors report teacher attendance at the
end of the third year as slightly better and

teacher turn-over as normal. Teacher attitudes toward education and teaching were found to be more positive and an increase in confidence was evidenced. Student attendance improved, and the number of discipline problems referred to the principal dropped by fifty percent. Data concerning achievement was not considered conclusive. Parent opinionnaires showed parents thought things went well during the first two years but decreased somewhat during the third year, although a majority of opinions were still positive.

Curriculum development resulted in content clusters being reduced from 16 to 3 (arts, humanities, and sciences) and interdisciplinary teams formed for each grade level. This process led to learning activities being developed and added to the curriculum.

Reporting to parents on student progress changed during the first year with further modifications the second and third year. The authors suspect these changes may have affected parent opinions of the program.

The authors describe the dissemination of program information as centering on the school community utilizing local media during the first and second years of the project. The third year dissemination focus was away from the local area towards regional and state-wide audiences which also may have been a reason for the lessening of confidence in the middle school by parents.

McGee and Krajewski report that their three year study of the transition of a school organization from a traditional junior high concept to that of a middle school raised many questions, answered some, and generated much data while providing a framework to view effectiveness and accomplishments. Their conclusion is that the middle school concept provides a better program for the emerging adolescent learner than the more traditional junior high school and evidence

224

indicates that the students and teachers involved
in this project would agree.

STUDENT PROGRESS IN SELF-PACED, COMPETENCY-BASED
    INDIVIDUALIZED SCIENCE CLASSES IN AN ALTERNATIVE
    PHILADELPHIA SCHOOL

Melton, A. Larry. Education, Volume 98, Summer
    1978, pp. 440-443.

Melton describes a competency-based curriculum
program operating in an alternative school that
stresses individualized and self-paced instruction.
The site of this program, Franklin Learning Center,
is a non-graded high school in Philadelphia that
provides continuous progress procedures in its
curriculum.

The author offered sequenced mini-courses to
two of his science classes enabling the students
to progress at their own rate of learning as they
mastered competencies. Competency is defined as
being able to demonstrate 80% proficiency in the
required content. Each mini-course was given a
value of one credit, and ten credits equaled one
Carnegie Unit. Because the school operates on a
continuous progress basis, students completed
course requirements in more or less time than it
would take in a traditional high school.

. During the first year of the program while
the students worked at their own rate, more than
half of the students completed sufficient mini-
course credits to equal one year's work in the
traditional curriculum, and after two years nearly
all had completed their work. Although the pace
was at a slower rate than in a traditional program,
competence averages were much higher as students
were required to achieve at least at the 80%
proficiency level.

Melton concludes that although students
require more time in a competency based program

to reach the set standards of performance, they do
acquire proficiency in subject area content before
being passed on to the next course or grade level.
He says, "students should attain credit based upon
performance standards rather than be passed on
from grade to grade merely due to their presence
in school." Other positive effects of the program
were observed such as a more relaxed atmosphere
and increased feelings of accomplishment among
students.

Melton concludes that both teachers and
administrators involved in continuous progress
programs based on student performance and competency
should be prepared for a seemingly slow rate of
learning. However, the overall atmosphere that
results from this type program is conducive to
teaching and learning as the students and teachers
work towards reachable goals based on immediate
past successes. The author identifies the most
important outcome as that of students assuming
responsibility for their own learning, a needed
and necessary step in the direction of becoming
a contributing member of society.

MODULAR INSTRUCTION IS THE WAY OF THE FUTURE

Radway, Bonnie and Betty Schroeder. Journal of
    Business Education, Volume 53, March 1978,
    pp. 247-250.

Radway and Schroeder describe a program that
utilizes modules of instruction to teach data
processing at the Capital Area Career Center in
Mason, Michigan. This area vocational center,
which serves eleven public high school districts,
developed the program to assist students gain
data processing skills necessary for employability.

Each module of instruction which they have
developed, constructed, and are using consists of
1) a performance objective, 2) pre-post tests,
3) a list of reading references, 4) a list of

materials and equipment needed to accomplish the task, 5) job steps to do the task, and 6) a technical word list. Some of the modules also use slides and tape media.

The modules were developed for the purpose of giving students the basic knowledge and hands-on skills needed for a specific entry level data processing job. To insure that the modules would do so, the program involved local industry employers who furnished actual job titles and job descriptions for data processing personnel whom they supervised. Employees in these positions then identified the job knowledge and skills necessary for their work including desirable attitudes and behaviors.

From this data, instructional modules were developed providing step by step instructions concerning specific tasks. Students progress at their own rate through the modules that teach the skills they will need for the specific job they want. Many modules concern knowledge in arithmetic, reading, and other basics that are a necessary base for many of the jobs involved. Sequences of learning have been established for each job desired by students,and therefore a student program consists of a series of modules beginning with the basic skills progressing into modules that integrate three or four skills. The next level of modules involves problem-solving situations called "trouble shooting" on the job. The final level of modules concerns transferring from hypothetical situations to actual on-the-job problems during which time students consult with other data processing workers and become involved in actual work.

The authors report unique modules have also been developed which orient students to career jobs in order that they can select a particular job for which they will receive training. These career decision-making modules pertain specifically to data processing and contain guest speakers from

227

the field, short hands-on experiences, and
proficiency tests in math, reading, and other
pre-employment skills.

Once a career choice has been made by the
student, the learning prescription is developed,
and the student receives a comprehensive list of
the modules to be completed. Weekly prescriptions
are then developed as the student progresses through
the modules at his own rate. The student receives
a computer print out of all the competencies
learned which can be used as credentials during
the job interviews.

Radman and Schroeder recognize success of the
program by 1) the enthusiasm of the students and
parents judged through participation and their
comments; 2) the continuing support and assistance
from employers who have provided materials, equipment, computer time, and personnel for assisting in
the training of students; 3) the excellent rate of
job placements; 4) the satisfaction employers have
indicated with graduates of the program they have
hired; 5) the movement of graduates up the career
ladder to more responsible jobs in data processing;
and 6) the fact that more than 60% of graduates
have gone on for further training.

FOUR-YEAR-OLDS IN SCHOOL?

Rosenberg, Leon A. Today's Education, Volume 68,
    September-October 1979, pp. 62-64.

Rosenberg reports on a study of educational
programs for four-year-olds in ten of Maryland's
school systems. This included 2,000 children in
33 early childhood education centers between 1973
and 1978. The purpose of the study was to determine
any cognitive and emotional changes that occurred
during the pre-kindergarten program and academic
skills acquired in kindergarten and first grade.

The study involved experimental and control
groups of children who were primarily from poor,

228

rural or urban families. The two groups were similar in background and at the same level of intellectual development at the beginning of the study. Both groups were given the same tests at the beginning and at the end of the pre-kindergarten program. The study or experimental group consisted of the children who were admitted to the pre-kindergarten program, and the control group consisted of children who did not attend such a program.

Data from the tests revealed that the study group showed social and emotional growth, but the control group did not. Also, the study group showed meaningful cognitive change. A follow-up of the children showed that the children who had participated in the pre-kindergarten programs continued to show outstanding growth through primary school. Rosenberg attributes these accomplishments to the successful pre-school programs which were directed by trained educators. They had basic educational goals and everyone expected to help the children increase their abilities.

Rosenberg concludes that there is a need for a firm commitment to make the education of the four-year-old an integral part of our educational system. However, he states that no one best educational model should be designated for this purpose.

TAKING THE SPECIAL OUT OF SPECIAL EDUCATION

Scherer, Marge. School and Community, Volume 64, March 1978, pp. 8-10.

Scherer presents an approach to mainstreaming in effect in Missouri, the Educational Resource Teacher (ERT), which is in compliance with federal regulations and Missouri law concerning educational provisions for the handicapped. The law states, "Impediments to learning and to normal function of such children (handicapped and severely handicapped) in the regular school environment shall be overcome whenever practicable by the provision of special aids and services rather than by separate schooling for the handicapped."

Seventy Missouri school districts have instituted special programs in accordance with the law. One hundred ten certified special education teachers have received ERT training, sixty of them through the federally-funded Project TIME (Teacher In-Service for Mainstream Education) at the University of Missouri-Columbia.

The ERT program provides techniques and materials for teachers who work with handicapped children who are mainstreamed in the regular classroom. The ERT program is not a total solution to all the problems of mainstreaming since federal law requires a full range of services for the handicapped to be instituted by 1980 in all schools receiving federal funds. The law also states that if the severity of the handicap cannot be met by supplementary classroom aids, those children will need special classes.

Several features of the ERT program are 1) provision of a lower per pupil expenditure for the mildly handicapped; 2) reimbursement of funds from state appropriations; 3) provision for in-service education to classroom teachers; and 4) training in screening, diagnosis, planning, and evaluating handicapped children.

Some criticisms or drawbacks of the ERT program are 1) limited direct teaching of handicapped children by the ERT, 2) possible delays in funding, 3) large volume of paperwork (developing IEP's - Individualized Education Programs - for each child and seeing that each is being implemented), 4) misunderstanding by regular classroom teachers, 5) ignoring the average child in favor of the handicapped, and 6) lack of preparation for these children to compete with the non-handicapped.

Persons involved in the ERT program see it as the organizational trend of the future because of the rapid mainstreaming taking place. The ERT is viewed as an intermediary between the child and the teacher, helping the handicapped child to adjust to the demands of the regular classroom.

VOLUNTARY INTEGRATION THROUGH THE ARTS

Stanley, Cheryl and Claude H. Cunningham. Kappa Delta Pi Record, Volume 14, October 1977, pp. 10 and 25.

Stanley and Cunningham describe Houston's Magnet School program with specific attention to how the arts are being used to assist voluntary integration. In order to curb "white flight" and declining student enrollment as well as to promote quality education, the Houston, Texas, School District began to implement the Magnet School Plan in 1975.

School officials supported the position that fine arts programs had great potential for attracting students based on the Magnet School concept. Special curricula were developed and implemented in 45 schools in order to attract, like a magnet, students of differing ethnic backgrounds. Ten of these schools have fine arts and music programs as their magnet attractions. Interested students were accepted in the magnet schools based on the ethnic ratio which reflected the district's overall ratio.

Each school was allowed to develop its own curriculum; therefore, no two schools' curricula are identical. The music magnet schools provide instruction in class piano (electronic piano labs), strings, band, chorus, and general music. Two of the music magnet schools have incorporated a full time art teacher in their curriculum. Subjects which may be found at the fine arts schools include general music, chorus, band, strings (including guitar), piano, speech/drama, art, dance, and

231

gymnastics. Three administrative organizational structures are evident in the ten magnet schools. They are add-on, school-within-a-school, and extended instructional day. Students choosing to attend a magnet school participate in the regular program as well as the magnet emphasis, thereby encountering an enriched general curriculum.

The authors report that at the close of the second year of the magnet school plan implementation, the music and fine arts magnet schools were successful in encouraging voluntary integration. The success of the program was also indicated by the large percentage of students expressing a desire to continue their music and fine arts activities.

AN ORIENTATION PROGRAM FOR A MIDDLE SCHOOL

Steltzer, W. N., Jr. Clearing House, Volume 52, May 1979, pp. 452-454.

Steltzer shows how the middle school in Avon Grove School District, West Grove, Pennsylvania orients incoming fifth graders to the middle grade organizational structure. Apprehension about this new environment with team teaching, intramurals, an extensive array of courses, and increased choice and freedom is lessened through a well planned series of experiences.

Parents, teachers, and fourth grade students of the two K-4 schools, and especially the school more removed from the middle school setting, were dismayed when the middle school was first built that these young children would move out of their "neighborhood" school to a far-away school located near an area of "roughnecks" and a variety of ethnic groups. Through the cooperation of the middle school and the two elementary school parent organizations, students are gradually oriented into the middle school organizational structure alleviating the fears of both the parents and students.

The initial phase of the orientation program is a visit of the middle school principal and two members of the Fifth Grade Student Cabinet to each fourth grade classroom. The fifth graders talk on subjects such as "How It Felt to Come to the Middle School" and "How It's Different from Fourth Grade." The fifth graders and the principal respond to questions of the fourth graders.

A few days later the fourth graders visit the middle school for an open discussion with the assistant principal and a tour of the building led by eighth graders. The following week an open house is held at the middle school for the parents and their fourth graders. A meeting held in the library with the principals and guidance counselor usually focuses on concerns about such things as bus transportation, gym lockers, and discipline policies with little attention to curriculum. This is followed by a tour of the building with the fourth graders showing their parents around.

In mid-May the fourth grade teachers complete a sectioning card on each student which is used by them and the middle school personnel in scheduling of students to the fall program. A field day for all fourth graders is held at the middle school sponsored by the elementary school parent organizations.

One week before the opening of school, new class lists are posted at the middle school. On the night before school resumes, the building is open for students and their parents to find their way around, check lockers, and visit the rooms where the students will go the next day. Big brothers and sisters are assigned, the second day of school, on a one to five basis with fifth graders excused from class-time to explore the school and get acquainted.

The orientation concludes with Open House at the end of September. Here parents attend their child's classes where teachers present their program of study and acquaint parents with goals, objectives, and teaching strategies.

Steltzer reports that parents, school people, and students now look forward to this change to a new school. They consider all activities of the orientation program well worth the time and effort. The community's estimate of the worth of the middle school is rising steadily.

OTHER REFERENCES

Beebe, Von N. "Spanish Comes Alive on la Isla
Caribe," Phi Delta Kappan, Volume 60, October
1978, pp. 95-98.

Block, Arthur R. "How to Handle Curriculum
Controversy: A Legal Perspective," National
Elementary Principal, Volume 57, January 1978,
pp. 35-41.

Coffman, Patricia L. "There Is a Simple Answer
to the Writing Problem," NASSP Bulletin,
Volume 62, February 1978, pp. 98-100.

Ford, Bonny E. "The Extended School Day:
Privilege, Not Punishment," Childhood Education,
Volume 53, April-May 1977, p. 298.

Gautier, Marjorie Jane, Nancy Brown, and William
A. Raisch. "Gateway to Growth: St. Louis
Adventure," Educational Leadership, Volume 35,
February 1978, pp. 384-389.

Hainen, Judith. "Make Room for Learning Centers,"
Music Educator Journal, Volume 63, January 1977,
pp. 47-49.

Hall, Kenneth D. and Virginia Brinson. "What About
Curriculum Reform at the State Level?"
Educational Leadership, Volume 35, February
1978, pp. 342-349.

Jennings, Wayne and Joe Nathan. "Startling/
Disturbing Research on School Program Effectiveness," Phi Delta Kappan, Volume 58, March 1978,
pp. 568-572.

Libbey, James K. "Eastern Kentucky's Learning Lab
Pays Off," Phi Delta Kappan, Volume 58, January
1977, p. 425.

Maeroff, Gene I. "Colleges Without Walls," Phi
Delta Kappan, Volume 60, April 1979, p. 573.

May, Jeffrey. "Personalized Self-Instruction at the Cambridge School," The Science Teacher, Volume 44, January 1977, pp. 22-23.

Moir, O. "Locally Identified Promising Programs: Quality Control Through Professional Judgment," Educational Leadership, Volume 36, October 1978, pp. 51-54.

Nordin, Virginia Davis and William Lloyd Turner. "More Than Segregation Academies: The Growing Protestant Fundamentalist Schools," Phi Delta Kappan, Volume 61, February 1980, pp. 391-394.

Ornstein, Allan C. "The Federal Role in Educational R & D," The Clearing House, Volume 51, January 1978, pp. 230-233.

Pincus, John and Richard C. Williams. "Planned Change in Urban School Districts," Phi Delta Kappan, Volume 60, June 1979, pp. 729-733.

Rich, Leslie. "A Process for Alternative Education," American Education, Volume 13, March 1977, pp. 23-26.

Smith, Jeffrey K. and Michael Katims. "Reading in the City: The Chicago Mastery Learning Reading Program," Phi Delta Kappan, Volume 59, November 1977, pp. 199-202.

Sullivan, Paul J. "Implementing Programs in Moral Education," Theory Into Practice, Volume 16, April 1977, pp. 118-123.

Trump, J. Lloyd and William Georgiades. "What Happened and What Did Not Happen in the Model Schools," NASSP Bulletin, Volume 61, May 1977, pp. 72-79.

Wong, Martin R., Beth Erickson, Patricia King, Jane Stoler, and Thomas Allen. "Perceptions and Activities in an Open Education Environment," Child Study Journal, Volume 7, Summer 1977, pp. 117-130.

CHAPTER X
CURRICULUM CONTENT

The curriculum of today is a far cry from the original structures of colonial times with the Bible as the primary text and reading, writing, and arithmetic as the content areas. In fact, the curriculum content has changed significantly in the last decade. Depending upon the structural constraints of the curriculum, many new courses have appeared or new topics have been integrated or infused into the regular courses. Such issues as health, art, music, careers, and sex were recognizable in earlier curriculum documents. But they have all gained significant attention and very creative designs in many school systems in recent years. Some topics receiving acknowledgement as important curricular needs in the 1970's for the first time include energy education, economic literacy, death, aging, cultural awareness, and science fiction. Depending on the intent and expectations of the person or persons interested in such topics, this content took the form of everything from a unit presented at one grade level to an elective course to a total curriculum component.

Curriculum content has been affected by innovations and modifications in both general and specialized areas. General education has been strengthened through innovative programs in career education, writing, reading, and basic arithmetic. Specialized courses in death education, music, fine arts, cultural pluralism, and foreign language have been modified to attain relevance for today's students. Another area receiving considerable attention has been the emphasis on environment, ecological, health, and energy education. Along with sex education, these are the socially conscious areas of the curriculum. In addition, courses in economics and social studies have increasingly emphasized social concern through school and community projects.

Career education emphasizes the development of appreciation for all vocations and professions and usually includes activities and experiences through which individuals prepare themselves for developing their careers. A positive career program is learner centered in goals, basic methodology, and evaluation. Career subjects are usually not taught as a separate subject but are used as a motivational technique in many classes. Career education may provide a way to include the arts and humanities for some of the activities students choose to do in their leisure time. Some basic understandings developed through the program include a knowledge of relevant subject matter, basic concepts, available community resources, and a disposition toward creativity and ingenuity.

The emphasis on environmental, ecological, and energy education seeks to improve the quality of life throughout the country and the world by fostering individual and social responsibility toward both natural and man-made environments. Environmental education is taught under a variety of names including outdoor education, nature study, field investigations, environmental arts, and pollution problems. Most of these topics can be adapted to rural, suburban, or urban settings. They are interdisciplinary in nature and frequently utilize workshop techniques. Many times governmental and private agencies assist schools in programs with an environmental or energy thrust.

There is a close relationship between the emphasis on health education and the programs in alcohol education, drug education, and sex education. Many educators are recommending an added emphasis in the area of health maintenance. Along with sex, drugs, and alcohol are studies in nutrition education, accident prevention, and disease prevention. Many of these topics are controversial in nature because feelings, attitudes, and values are involved along with the cognitive content. Using alcohol education as an example

238

of this category of content, a typical program
might include study of the definition of alcohol,
the existence of negative attitudes, the increased
incidence of alcoholism among the young, treatment
alternatives, and the role of education in alcohol
problems.

Increased attention is being given to moral
education, religion, values, aging, and death
education. Since these topics are closely
related, they are being treated in an interdisciplinary nature involving both the cognitive
and affective domains. Many parents view these
topics as encroaching upon the responsibilities of
home and church while other parents say that these
topics are definitely a part of the school curriculum. As an example of the inherent difficulties
of incorporating these topics into the curriculum,
moral education serves as a pertinent illustration.
Many educators agree that moral education is a
necessity for public education, but from this
initial position many factors have to be taken
into account. These include teacher training for
moral education, a curriculum plan in the schools
to accommodate moral education, and the question
of general public acceptance of a moral education
program.

Consumer and economics programs in the curriculum are reflections of current society. These
topics usually deal with information which is
helpful to students on a practical level. Many
times these courses are tied in with career
education. These topics cannot be confined to
the classroom. Field trips to various industrial
and business concerns provide opportunity for
learning about the practical application of the
American economic system. As students become
more aware of consumer/economics practices, they
can develop attitudes of self-reliance and
knowledge of money matters.

The move toward cultural pluralism is
reflected in the emphases in foreign language
instruction on the cultural, ethnic, and

linguistic traits of various groups. Foreign
language students experience the feelings and
pride of the group's language they are mastering.
A key factor is to provide students with curriculum
opportunities which present an awareness of other
cultural groups while retaining their own cultural
heritage.

Many teachers are also revising and strengthening their basic content courses. This has been
exemplified by the back-to-the-basics movement and
the increased emphasis on reading, writing, and
speaking at all grade levels. These fundamental
content areas are experiencing a modified reform
movement around the country. A major objective is
the development of processes whereby a student
becomes stronger in communication areas. Much
of the new content is being incorporated into the
discipline areas of English, mathematics, science,
and history. In a similar manner, the fields of
music, arts, and physical education are strengthening
their programs through innovation and revision.

The study of the future through the utilization of science fiction and other means is appearing
in some schools with the rationale that understanding present trends will assist in improving future
solutions to problems. Futuristic settings which
involve cultural and societal problems are studied
along with the present and past to arrive at
solutions for improved living conditions. By
capturing the interest and curiosity of students,
futuristic studies become a vehicle for improving
present societal problems.

Many curriculum content changes have been
affected by textbook revisions and innovative
teacher education programs. This double-barreled
approach, new textbooks and new teachers with
enthusiastic plans, has provided the basis for
much curriculum content revision during the past
decade. The new teachers and the new text
materials have been assisting students by making
content more relevant and practical both in academic
and occupational areas of the curriculum.

In summary, a study of current curriculum content developments indicates that revised and innovative approaches are being tried and tested in various locations in the nation. These programs have been characterized by the strengthening of content and skills through the basics such as reading, writing, speaking, and numerical concepts. Cognitive and affective learnings are being merged in the areas of career education, sex education, health education, energy education, ecological education, futures education, and other content areas. The capability to relate content to attitudes is gaining increased status at all grade levels. Skills in content process and human relations are appearing with some frequency. The combined efforts of educators, parents, and students insure a strengthening of the curriculum content of the schools through effective planning, implementation, and evaluation.

SYNOPSES

THE HEALTH CURRICULUM: FILL IN THE BLANK

Barron, Melanie. National Elementary Principal,
    Volume 57, March 1978, pp. 78-84.

Barron reports that based upon an ERIC
search few if any comprehensive interdisciplinary
K-12 health education programs are in existence.
However, there are many outstanding programs at
national and local levels which deal with the
various facets of health education.

At the national level, Barron describes five
programs: 1) The Health Activities Project (HAP),
an activity centered, supplementary program for
fifth to eighth grade students; 2) The School
Health Curriculum Project, an organized, highly
structured, sequential course aimed at preventive
education about smoking for use in elementary and
primary grades; 3) Project Burn Prevention using
education as an intervention strategy to increase
knowledge and appropriate behaviors and attitudes
to reduce the number and severity of burns;
4) The School Health Education Study which
organized over forty health topics into ten basic
concepts, each aimed at attaining behavioral goals;
and 5) The Comprehensive School/Community Health
Education Project (CS/CHE) which aims at increasing
community awareness and understanding of health
education needs and resources and developing
support for more effective health education for
adults and young people in schools and the
general community.

At the local level, the author describes four
projects: 1) The UCLA "self care" program which
attempts to involve children in making decisions
about their own health problems; 2) California's
Secondary School's Allied Health Pilot and
Demonstration Project aimed at relating life
sciences and health studies to real situations,
occupations, and tasks through cooperative
community effort; 3) The Cardiovascular Curriculum
Education Project (CCEP) designed to increase

knowledge and awareness among ninth and tenth
graders of the risk factors associated with
cardiovascular disease through self-paced
instruction; and 4) The New York University-
Joan of Arc Cooperative Education Program
involving eighth and ninth grade students in
a program of science activities and individual
placement with health professionals in all fields
of the basic medical sciences.

Barron lists several sources of text and
resource materials including The Curriculum
Advisory Service and Health Education: A Resource
Handbook for Teachers. She concludes with a
description of the key role played by the principal
in developing health education in an elementary
and a junior high school.

NO ONLOOKERS ALLOWED

Beachy, William. Music Educators Journal, Volume
    63, April 1977, pp. 50-51.

Beachy reports on an Introduction to Instrumental Music Study in Howard County, Maryland. He
states that in most elementary schools, students
introduced to instruments are often encouraged to
study them through demonstration performances by
professional musicians, high school musicians,
faculty members, or local music instrument dealers.
The Introductory Instrumental Music Program
allowed the students to learn about instruments
by actually playing them. This pilot program gave
every child in grades four and five an opportunity
to play the trumpet, violin, drums, and clarinet.

Each homeroom class engaged in band instruction for a thirty-minute period each week. They
played the drums for the first nine weeks, then
the trumpets, violins, and clarinets for nine
weeks each. The students played songs in groups
accompanied by the instructor on the piano. After
this procedure they volunteered to play solo or
with their friends. The major instructor

responsibility in the program was the selection of material. Care was taken to ensure that music was immediately played by the beginner and that the material was not too technical. During the first nine weeks the students played selections on the drums that were written specifically for the program. For the other instruments, the material selected was primarily derived from standard method books.

It was hoped that they would be better able to choose which instrument they might like to play. It also provided students with opportunities to handle and hear other instruments in a particular family being studied and to obtain information about various types of instrumental groups such as chamber, ensemble, and concert.

THE ARTS: SENSORY WAYS OF LEARNING AND KNOWING

Brigham, Don L. NASSP Bulletin, Volume 63, November 1979, pp. 12-18.

Brigham describes the visual arts curriculum in the public schools of Attleboro, Massachusetts. This program is titled "Visual Arts in Basic Education." This curriculum focuses upon student acquisition and application of a set of educationally fundamental visual concepts. These visual or multi-sensory concepts are basic knowledge structures in other subjects of the school curriculum.

Brigham reports that through the concerted effort of many teachers and administrators, a guidebook was designed and edited to meet the needs of the visual arts curriculum. The visual concepts of the elementary, middle, and high school levels have been listed and defined in the Attleboro guidebook. Five concepts are listed for the elementary program. These concepts are valuing; perceiving, analyzing, forming, and expressing part-to-whole relationships; transformational change processes in the natural and constructed world; and relationships of form to function in natural and constructed things. Middle-school art teachers agreed upon these basic conceptual categories: point, line, color, sequence, texture, intersection, balance, form, motion, figure-ground, abstraction, depth, basic structures, closure, visual analogy, and self concept. The high school concepts are observation/representation, abstraction, improvisation, visual analogy, design elements, organizational principles, environmental exploration, wholeness, expressive form, visual metaphor, synthesis, qualitative criteria for art, and developing individual style.

These concepts are taught through various art lessons at different levels of education. Brigham states that the concepts of Visual Arts in Basic Education are taught sensorily and experientially rather than verbally.

The author reports that a 1977-78 evaluation of the visual arts program was conducted at the seventh grade level. Text questions were devised, and pre- and post-tests were administered to Attleboro students and to a control group in a comparable community. The test results were significant in favor of the Attleboro students.

ARTS ALIVE IN GREENWICH

Davenport, Benjamin. NASSP Bulletin, Volume 63, November 1979, pp. 55-57.

Davenport, principal of Eastern Junior High School in Greenwich, Connecticut, describes how his school pays tribute to cultural arts by having gifted artists from New York "take over" the school for a day by working, demonstrating, or performing with and for the student.

"Arts Alive" became a one-day program in which fifty artists from fields of music, ballet, opera, sculpture, painting, theater, writing, announcing, photography, instrument-making, and

cartooning volunteered to teach classes or involve
teachers in workshops. A citizens' group, the
Greenwich Arts Council, helped find artists who
would volunteer their time free of charge. Planning, scheduling, programming, and constant
communication with the artists were vital to
make the day successful.

The nine hundred students in the seventh,
eighth, and ninth grades at Eastern received a
nine-page guide to "Arts Alive" in January. Each
student then chose ten programs from the fifty
offered that are described in detail. A group
of parents then helped with scheduling the
students into the courses. Excellent publicity
was arranged by a P.T.A. committee. However,
the enthusiasm of eighth and ninth grade students
who had attended "Arts Alive" the previous year
was the best publicity to the seventh graders,
parents, and the community-at-large.

MEANINGFUL CAREER EDUCATION IN THE MIDDLE SCHOOL

Duff, Charles F. NASSP Bulletin, Volume 62, April
    1978, pp. 60-63.

Duff recognizes that career education programs
often fail to provide the student with a clear-cut
lifelike picture of what the working world is
really like. A "Person to Person" program
developed in a middle school is presented as a
means of overcoming this deficiency.

The program gives a student a chance to visit
and talk directly with a person actively engaged
in a career which has caught the student's interest.
Five steps are taken in the "Person to Person"
process. The student identifies his career choice
and is aided by the counselor in forming questions
to be asked during the on-site visit. The
counselor locates an appropriate resource person
and arranges for the visit during the school day.
Finally, the student and counselor engage in a
follow-up interview to evaluate the visit.

The author states that there are many benefits
from the program. The student gains first hand
experience and knowledge and serves as a positive
agent for the school. Also, the students develop
favorable impressions toward the adults who have
taken the time to assist them.

Duff concludes that a "Person to Person"
program can work almost anywhere as long as two
essential criteria are met. These are a willingness to search out the persons in the community
to develop a resource file, and a willingness to
take the time needed for planning and implementation.

HOW WE IMPROVED OUR SEX EDUCATION PROGRAM

Edgemon, Albert W. and William R. Thomas.
    Educational Leadership, Volume 37, December
    1979, pp. 256-258.

The authors describe the process used in
developing a new sex and family life curriculum
for fifth and sixth graders in the Falls Church,
Virginia, schools. Parents were surveyed to
determine what kind of program was needed,
supportable, and desirable. Positive response
was reported from the twenty-two percent of the
surveys returned, with only five of the forms
indicating any negative responses.

According to Edgemon and Thomas, data from the
survey were used by a curriculum council to develop
a procedure for implementation including a philosophy statement, program guidelines, and basic
concepts. Basic concepts germane to the content
and materials of instruction outlined were (1) the
body is an interrelated whole, (2) the endocrine
system influences growth and development, (3) all
human beings have developed from a joining of a
male spermatozoa and female egg, and (4) relationships with family and peers change as people
mature. Procedures followed in implementation of
the sex and family life curriculum involved adding

247

to the curriculum council parents, religious leaders, and health and medical professionals in addition to the school personnel. The school board, working with principals, took steps to insure parent involvement in program development and to see that means of keeping them informed were provided.

Edgemon and Thomas report that the program as presented to sixth graders the first year was evaluated positively by students with no negative input on the part of parents. The authors conclude that the program's success resulted from consideration of nine strategic points including identification of a tangible need on which to focus general concern, use of expert opinion in terms of specific subject matter and instructional processes, and use of a leader with both personal interest and general credibility among staff and community.

MATHEMATICS EDUCATION - 1955-1975: A SUMMARY OF THE FINDINGS

Gibney, Thomas and Edward Karns. Educational Leadership, Volume 36, February 1979, pp. 356-359.

Gibney and Karns report on a National Science Foundation survey on mathematics education over a 20 year period. According to the study, mathematics instruction changed very little from 1955 to 1975. The national study revealed mostly traditional content, textbook teaching, and little supervision. Also, the self-contained classroom at the elementary level and the fixed period schedule of the secondary school are still the predominant patterns for mathematics instruction.

Gibney and Karns surveyed the literature and utilized case studies to study content, "new math," back to basics, instructional strategies, classroom size/management, evaluation, inquiry teaching, and materials. Some of the more interesting findings were 1) the most frequently taught secondary courses include general math, algebra, and geometry while elementary instruction had expanded from arithmetic to geometry measurement, probability/statistics, graphs, equations, and other topics; 2) despite the "new math" thrust, and although the number and variety of math courses increased since 1955, there appeared to be little change in mathematics instruction in K-12 levels; 3) teachers have been and are still stressing basic mathematics skills at all grade levels; 4) by 1975, the pendulum seemed to be swinging back to one teaching source - the textbook; 5) the size of the group with which the teacher works on a particular topic may be of importance; 6) articulation between elementary and secondary seemed to be a universal problem; 7) the use of standardized tests was more common in math than in science or social science; 8) the greatest change in testing over the past 20 years has been the concern for criterion-referenced tests rather than norm-referenced tests; and 9) mathematics teachers and instruction remains rather traditional with little emphasis on inquiry teaching.

Gibney and Karns conclude by listing critical areas of teaching performance relating to how instruction is organized, how materials are used, and how much time is spent in direct instruction. Further, leadership to provide adequate supervision for mathematics teachers is critical.

TEACHING ABOUT AGING

Glass, J. Conrad and Curtis Trent. High School Journal, Volume 63, November 1979, pp. 80-82.

Glass and Trent report on a study in nine North Carolina Schools designed to determine if attitudes of youth toward older persons could be changed. Based on the negative conception of old age generally formed among young people, a study unit consisting of 10 fifty-minute sessions was developed.

Using an attitude toward older persons scale developed by N. Kogan, 451 ninth grade social studies students were found to have about the same attitudes toward older persons. The unit on aging was taught by local teachers to a section of students, known as the treatment group, in each school while one section of similar students in each school where the unit was taught served as the control groups.

The unit on aging included such topics as Myths and Realities of Aging, What Will I Be Like When I Get Old, and Young and Old Getting Together. A variety of techniques and media was used to help the students sense some of the problems older people encounter such as impaired hearing and vision. They were also able to talk with some of the more accomplished, happy, and alert older people. Specific attention was directed toward enabling the young people to "understand the relationship between how one lives one's life and the kind of person one becomes as he or she grows old."

According to the authors, a posttest was given to the treatment groups and the control groups at the end of the two-week study and four to six months later. They report that there was a significant change at both test periods in attitude toward older persons on the part of the students in the treatment groups. In addition to the positive influence of the study unit on attitude change, the students found the materials to be interesting and informative.

The authors surmise, based on findings of this study, that periodic encounters with positive factors about aging throughout the public school years of students would result in more positive attitudes toward older persons and toward one's own aging. They also suggest that techniques applied in this study might be used in many situations where attitude change is desirable.

THE REBIRTH OF FOREIGN LANGUAGES IN THE ELEMENTARY
    SCHOOL

Met, Myriam. Educational Leadership, Volume 37,
    January 1980, pp. 321-323.

    Met presents specific examples to show the quiet revolution in the return of foreign language instruction to the elementary school curriculum despite the indifference toward second language study. This indifference has been characterized by poor financial support and lack of professional interest at K-12 levels and post-secondary levels. The enthusiasm of the 1950s and 1960s for Foreign Language in the Elementary School (FLES) has greatly diminished, but the author describes the new movement as one which has received its impetus from diverse sources. These sources include a focus on the ethnic heritage of cultural minorities, the emphasis on bilingual education, and the magnet school movement. Met describes current programs in California, Montreal, St. Louis, Cincinnati, and Chicago.

    In California, English speaking students in Culver City, San Diego, and Hayward are taught their regular school subjects in Spanish. One of the earliest and best known bilingual programs was the St. Lambert experiment in Montreal in which English speaking students became fluent in French. The students were "immersed" in French starting in kindergarten. These total immersion programs in a foreign language have been utilized in at least four locations in the United States. The public schools of St. Louis, Cincinnati, and Chicago all offer foreign language through magnet schools. As one example, the Lasalle Language Academy in Chicago is an exemplary school.

251

Lasalle is a magnet school designed to attract K-8
students to a racially balanced language learning
center that is part of Chicago's Access to
Excellence program. The school offers Spanish,
French, German, Italian, and English as a second
language to a somewhat academically diverse
school population. The elementary school language
program articulates with a high school language
center.

Met concludes that a new period of growth in
elementary school foreign language instruction is
occurring at the present time with a wide variety
of old and new models to choose from. The author
foresees affective education and values clarification as a part of some elementary foreign
language courses. Multinational business corpo-
rations and multicultural education also have
influenced this resurgence of elementary foreign
language teaching.

ANATOMY COURSE GIVES WYOMING STUDENTS A HEAD START
    ON MEDICINE

Ohio Schools, Volume 56, October 1978, pp. 16-18.

When she learned that her former biology
students who had gone into various medical fields
were lacking in their anatomy background, Wyoming
(Cincinnati, Ohio) High School teacher Marie King
began a new course in human anatomy. The course
is open only to seniors considering a medical
career, and competition to get into the course
is described as increasingly "fierce." Students
are selected on the basis of grades and the number
of advanced science courses they have already
completed. Once enrolled in the course, seniors
have an excellent opportunity to decide whether
or not a medical career is really what they want
to pursue.

King's approach to the course is to prepare
students intensively in a particular area of

anatomy and then take them on after-school field trips to local hospitals, the University of Cincinnati Medical School, and doctors' offices. Occasionally doctors come to the high school to lecture to King's class. King's students are able to assist medical students dissecting cadavers, watch surgeons perform surgery, and hear specialists discuss their fields. Doctors frequently invite students who are particularly interested in their fields to spend Saturdays observing them in their work. Doctors have further assisted by donating hundreds of medical books for the students' use, and the school board has cooperated by purchasing much expensive equipment.

Students are assigned one disease a month to research and submit a pathology report. The report must include a definition of the disease, its etiology, a blood picture, how to test for it, and its treatment.

King says that although the success of her anatomy course is partially dependent on the fact that there are many doctors in the Wyoming High School community, almost any school could develop a course similar to hers if the science teacher would utilize available resources such as hospitals and doctors.

CLASSROOM MINI-SOCIETY HELPS YOUNGSTERS LEARN
   ABOUT ECONOMICS

Ohio Schools, Volume 56, February 1978, p. 16.

This is a report on a successful program instigated during the 1977-78 academic year at Kent Elementary School in Columbus, Ohio. About 90 students at Kent took part in the year-long program designed to help them learn how to function as job-holders, consumers, investors, and savers. The students, led by three teachers and two resource persons, were part of a mini-society

253

created at Kent to teach them economics and the free enterprise system. The students spent three to four hours a week studying in their mini-society. Their studies consisted of field trips, class discussions, projects, and actual business ventures.

Part of the effort to help the students learn about job opportunities was teaching them to fill out job applications. When a student wanted to join the school safety patrol or work in the office, for example, he had to complete a job application form. Additionally, workers in many professions and fields came to talk to the students about their jobs.

One of the most interesting aspects of the program was that students learned to set up an economic society. A Columbus bank arranged for a tour and a joint savings account for student deposits. The bank printed facsimile checks for the students and a facsimile currency for them to buy goods and services in their mini-society. Students decided on projects to make money, and profits were deposited in their savings account. Some students volunteered to act as bank tellers and record keepers. Students could borrow and withdraw money as well as make deposits. Interest earned by the savings was to be equitably divided at the end of the school year.

Some rewards of the project besides teaching economic literacy were that students became involved with their families when they asked for help in setting up personal budgets, they developed better self concepts, and they learned much about decision-making and cooperation. The program met with so much success that at the time this article was published, the program originators planned to continue it indefinitely.

SCIENCE FICTION IN THE 7-12 CURRICULUM

Reynolds, John C., Jr. The Clearing House, Volume
    51, November 1977, pp. 121-125.

    Reynolds investigates the use of science
fiction in grades 7-12 classroom instruction. Three
hundred teachers were surveyed in four southeastern
states during two academic years. The survey data
include 1) disciplines using science fiction
2) basic themes of science fiction, and 3) teacher
comments about science fiction in the curriculum.
Of the three hundred teachers surveyed, 177 used
science fiction in their curriculums including
seventy percent in grades 10-12 and thirty percent
in grades 7-9. Science fiction appeared most
frequently in literature followed by biology,
science, history, health, and English. Science
fiction was used less in art, chemistry, physics,
music, and math.

    The increase in use of science fiction in
the classroom was attributed to students watching
movies such as, 2001: A Space Odyssey, The
Illustrated Man, Fahrenheit 451, and The Time
Machine. These movies stimulated teachers to
utilize techniques of building models of cities
of the future, seeing earth through alien eyes,
and inventing a planet or spaceship for human use.
Science fiction short stories and novels were used
in reading and writing assignments.

    The survey revealed three basic themes or
categories: 1) hard science fiction dealing with
gadgets, computers, and predictive themes;
2) social science fiction which focused on human
activities in areas such as psychology, anthropology,
political systems, and theology themes; and 3) science
fantasy encompassing way-out alternative universes,
anti-matter galaxies, and other themes which
deviate from natural laws and theories.

    Reynolds says students of grades 7-12 are
stimulated most by science fiction because of its

mass recognition through television, films, and books. Many teachers have capitalized on its positive benefits through reading and writing assignments which are based on student interests and curiosity.

SOWING SEEDS OF PROMISE: TO CREATE MEANINGFUL
    CONTEXTS FOR SKILLS

Shaughnessy, John. Educational Leadership, Volume
    36, December 1978, pp. 203-205.

Shaughnessy refutes the flaunted position that schools have shelved attention to basic skills, particularly those in language arts, citizenship, and computation. He says that "quality school programming continuously incorporates the best of the new and promising with the most valued and valuable of the old." His concern is that under duress for producing students who are more knowledgeable in the skills, unrelated drill in excess may mitigate against the objective of actually being able to use a skill in societal situations. For example, too often the assumption is that writing is being taught because skills used in writing are being taught. However, research shows that knowledge of grammar has no effect on writing.

Shaughnessy cites several examples of programs in which students develop basic skills in connection with meaningful activities. He says this list, chosen from many examples, is demonstrative of the fact that learning and reinforcement of important basic skills is being accomplished.

The Weehawken (New Jersey) Individualized Language Arts program presents a language-experience approach with the techniques derived from modern linguistic theory to enhance children's writing. It encourages the development of writing in all subject areas of the curriculum and plots growth against a set of clearly defined objectives.

The Parkway School District in St. Louis County, Missouri, has designed a seventh- and eighth-grade unified studies program (language arts, social studies, and reading) in which basic skill treatment is an integral part of the day's lesson.

A writers-in-the-schools program in the Ladue School District (St. Louis, Missouri) brought published authors into the classroom to work with students on creative writing. The program produced an anthology which demonstrated the integration of lower order skills in writing.

Twenty ninth grade science students spent five days at the Koster Dig in Illinois as student archaeologists. These students went through the entire sequence of events involved in an archaeological dig, and in the process applied a variety of important basic skills.

ACES, A COMMUNITY EDUCATION PROGRAM

Somerville, Thomas. NASSP Bulletin, Volume 61, April 1977, pp. 116-118.

For the past two years Frederick Roehm Junior High School, Berea, Ohio, has arranged an Academic and Cultural Events Series for students. Developing student awareness is a primary goal of the series (ACES). It is the first occasion for many students to experience theater and ballet or to visit places other than those in their immediate home-school area. Learning to react as a member of an adult audience is for many students a new venture.

ACES is an effort to develop a multi-curricular program. This approach allows students to attain basic skills and to gain insight and experience that can be used for making appropriate educational and vocational choices. The program provides the means for a very personalized education for each student.

The lists of events for ACES is developed several months before the spring quarter when the series begins. The faculty suggests events relevant to their subject area; area colleges, chambers of commerce, and other local sources are contacted for ideas; and students suggest activities. The final list offers something of interest in many different areas.

A variety of activities have been available for student participation and selection in the two years of the program, including: the Cleveland Art Museum, a visit to the Federal Building including a court case, a ballet performance at Akron State University, a Cleveland Indians game; the Ice Follies, a Bach music concert, and services in a Jewish temple.

A list of thirty activities are selected each year. Each activity is designed to accommodate from 100 to 125 students. Each student selects a minimum of ten events.

A seminar is scheduled once a week to prepare students for the events scheduled that week and to review past events. The response to the program has been positive. Data indicate that the program has broadened the educational background of the students by exposing them to events and places with which they normally would not have come into contact. Helping the students to mature socially, fostering an appreciation for the arts and other skills of man, and promoting self-discipline and responsibility are key benefits derived from the program.

A READING PROGRAM FOR THE HIGH SCHOOL

Stone, Clarence and Rita Riddle. NASSP Bulletin, Volume 62, February 1978, pp. 121-122.

Stone, principal at Highland Park High School, Highland Park, Michigan, and Riddle, reading consultant at the same school, describe a reading improvement program at the high school level. A reading lab using the Random House High Intensity Training (HIT) System was instigated in the school. HIT System is an instructional management program that utilizes many different reading programs. It is an individualized, multilevel, flexible program that uses a variety of materials.

With the HIT System teachers are able to diagnose the students' reading needs and prescribe appropriate materials and activities to meet those needs. The system has 400 reading objectives divided into four categories: vocabulary, word study, comprehension, and study skills. Each category has multilevel activities to fit the span of objectives for the non-reader and the good reader. For example, audio materials are listed for a learner who learns through listening, programmed materials for more independent learners, and workbook type materials for the visual learners. The HIT System is flexible enough to allow the teacher to plan group activities when needed. When students master prescribed objectives, they are given different types of rewards.

The teachers and counselors recommend ninth and tenth grade students to be tested for the special reading program. Then the building reading consultant schedules them into a reading lab which is a full-year course and an alternative to English. The consultant provides continuous aid to former reading lab students by instructing English teachers in the use of content area reading techniques. She also supplies supplemental material for English teachers. The school plans to extend reading consultant services to social studies, math, and science in the future.

HOW WRITING ISN'T - BUT SHOULD BE - TAUGHT IN AMERICAN SCHOOLS

Tibbetts, Arn M. and Charlene Tibbetts. Educational Leadership, Volume 37, March 1980, pp. 478-480.

The Tibbetts share their findings and concerns about the teaching of writing based on visits to 50 schools in all major regions of the country. Their major objective was to find evidence that would relate test scores and teaching. They report that no solid evidence of this relationship was found; however, they "discovered plenty about the way writing is taught - or isn't taught - in American schools."

In response to questions asked teachers about what new ideas are being used that work and what has influenced teaching in the last 20 years, teachers responded that nothing has changed. Essentially the same response came from college writing teachers and public school administrators. As to why this stalemate, the Tibbetts found that the researchers who write and theorize belong to one class while teachers belong to another. They say that "teachers and writers fail to communicate because of an enormous difference in how they must live their daily lives." An example of this is the new grammars that came from the universities. "Students could not learn it, and teachers could not understand it well enough to teach it."

A second example of this statement came to light when a sample of teachers visited by the Tibbetts agreed to take the ACT English Usage Test. These experienced teachers "did no better than our own college English education majors." The teachers claimed "they taught the grammatical operations on the test, but they could not consistently answer the questions right!"

Who is to blame? The Tibbetts say the situation is an American cultural problem for which the schools alone can not be blamed. However, if professionals are to be blamed, teacher trainers in college and school administrators are the most vulnerable.

The Tibbetts have made several recommendations for coping with this American problem. They would

have college professors be more practical in
their teaching; have English textbooks which
present English as it is actually spoken and
written; move forward with the "basics," not
"back;" use drill in the classroom more effectively; encourage teachers to grade harder;
have teachers write; start a state association
for practical composition; and have strong,
capable, sympathetic principals who support
the effective use of language.

OTHER REFERENCES

Blaufarb, Marjorie. "As I See Coed Physical Education," Today's Education, Volume 67, April-May 1978, pp. 54-56.

Clements, Mary. "Health and Drug Education -- A Regional Approach," Educational Leadership, Volume 35, January 1978, pp. 314-317.

Coffman, Patricia L. "There Is a Simple Answer to the Writing Problem," NASSP Bulletin, Volume 62, February 1978, pp. 98-100.

Cortes, Carlos E. "The Societal Curriculum and the School Curriculum: Allies or Antagonists?" Educational Leadership, Volume 36, April 1979, pp. 475-479.

Duet, Claude P., and John Newfield. "Labor: An Untapped Resource in Career Education," NASSP Bulletin, Volume 62, April 1978, pp. 50-59.

Egan, Dieran. "Attitude Formation and Social Studies Teaching," The Clearing House, Volume 53, January 1980, pp. 213-216.

Finn, P. "Integrating Career Education Into Subject Area Classrooms," NASSP Bulletin, Volume 62, April 1978, pp. 64-70.

Fitzner, Dale H. and Jean C. Rush. "The Arts Education Collaborative: Tucson's Model Arts Advocacy Program," NASSP Bulletin, Volume 63, November 1979, pp. 65-69.

Gray, James and Miles Myers. "The Bay Area Writing Project," Phi Delta Kappan, Volume 59, February 1978, pp. 410-413.

Holliday, Frances B. and Carole Edwards. "Building on Cultural Strengths: A Route to Academic Achievement," Educational Leadership, Volume 36, December 1978, pp. 207-210.

Hymovitz, Leon. "Death As a Discipline: The Ultimate Curriculum," NASSP Bulletin, Volume 63, February 1979, pp. 102-106.

Ponder, Gerald. "The More Things Change ...: The Status of Social Studies," Educational Leadership, Volume 36, April 1979, pp. 515-518.

Robinson, Carol M. "Developmental Counseling Approach to Death and Dying Education," Elementary School Guidance and Counseling, Volume 12, February 1978, pp. 178-187.

Roller, L. W. "Career Education: An Alternative High School Program," NASSP Bulletin, Volume 62, April 1978, pp. 47-49.

Rosenthal, Nina R. "Death Education: Help or Hurt," The Clearing House, Volume 53, January 1980, pp. 224-226.

Rossman, Jean F. "How One High School Set Up a Reading Program for 500 Students," Journal of Reading, Volume 20, February 1977, pp. 393-397.

Rottier, Jerry. "A New Approach to Teaching Mathematics," NASSP Bulletin, Volume 62, October 1979, pp. 61-65.

Rucker, Margaret E., Leslie M. Thompson, and Ben E. Dickerson. "Puppet Life and Death Education," The Clearing House, Volume 51, May 1978, pp. 458-459.

Schneider, Donald O. and Mary Jo McGee Brown. "Helping Students Comprehend Their Social Studies Textbooks," Social Education, Volume 44, February 1980, pp. 105-112.

Thompson, Margery. "How Schools Are Helping Kids Who Can't Speak English," The American School Board Journal, Volume 167, April 1980, pp. 35-39.

EPILOGUE

The authors are aware of the various concerns surrounding the identification and dissemination of trend lists or studies. They understand that any stated list is dependent upon the selection of process and literature for study as well as the interests and concerns of the investigators. The trends and issues reported in this publication represent the results of systematic analysis of over one thousand selected journal articles published since 1977.

Similar studies have been conducted periodically in an effort to document changes in educational practices since 1964. Findings from the previous studies and information about the processes involved in gaining data for these studies are recorded in the publications listed below.

Textbooks:

> Wootton, Lutian R., and John C. Reynolds, Jr. Trends Influence Curriculum, MSS Information Corporation, New York, 1972. 321 pages.

> Wootton, Lutian R., and John C. Reynolds, Jr. Trends Influence Curriculum, MSS Information Corporation, New York, 1974. 266 pages.

> Wootton, Lutian R., and John C. Reynolds, Jr. Trends and Issues Affecting Curriculum, University Press of America, Washington, D.C., 1977. 139 pages.

Journal Articles:

> Wootton, Lutian R., John C. Reynolds, Jr., and Jerald M. Bullock. "Trends Affecting Curriculum 1964-1974," Educational

Leadership, Volume 32, January 1975, pp. 286-289.

Wootton, Lutian R., John C. Reynolds, Jr., and Charles S. Gifford. "Modified Educational Emphases Revealed Through Professional Journals," Contemporary Education, Volume 48, Winter 1977, pp. 101-105.

Gifford, Charles S., Lutian R. Wootton, and John C. Reynolds, Jr. "A Study of Educational Trends: Product, Process, and By-Products," Kappa Delta Pi Record, Volume 14, April 1978, pp. 99-100.

Wootton, Lutian R., John C. Reynolds, Jr., and Charles S. Gifford. "An Institution Responds to Student Needs for Knowledge of Educational Innovations," Contemporary Education, Volume 50, April 1979, pp. 166-168.